HERETIC!

An LGBTQ-Affirming, Divine Violence-Denying,
Christian Universalist's Responses to Some of
Evangelical Christianity's Most Pressing Concerns

MATTHEW J. DISTEFANO

All rights reserved. No part of this book may be used or reproduced, stored in a retrieval system, or transmitted in any form or by any means, electronic, mechanical, photocopying, recording, scanning, or otherwise, without written permission from the publisher except in the case of brief quotations embodied in critical articles and reviews. Permission for wider usage of this material can be obtained through Quoir by emailing permission@quoir.com.

Copyright © 2018 by Matthew J. Distefano.

First Edition

Cover design and layout by Rafael Polendo (polendo.net)

Scripture quotations, unless otherwise noted, taken from the *New Revised Standard Version* and are copyright © 1989 by the Division of Christian Education of the National Council of Churches of Christ in the U.S.A. and are used by permission.

Scriptures marked KJV are taken from the *King James Version* (KJV): *King James Version*, public domain.

Scripture texts marked NAB are taken from the *New American Bible, revised edition* © 2010, 1991, 1986, 1970 Confraternity of Christian Doctrine, Washington, D.C. and are used by permission of the copyright owner. All rights reserved.

Scriptures marked NKJV are taken from the *New King James Version* (NKJV): Scripture taken from the *New King James Version*®. Copyright © 1982 by Thomas Nelson, Inc. Used by permission. All rights reserved.

ISBN 978-1-938480-30-0

This volume is printed on acid free paper and meets ANSI Z39.48 standards. Printed in the United States of America

Published by Quoir
Orange, California

www.quoir.com

Dedication

To Lyndsay and Elyse, Michael and Speri,
and everyone else who believes in me

Table of Contents

FOREWORD BY MICHELLE COLLINS 7

PREFACE 11

ACKNOWLEDGEMENTS 13

INTRODUCTION 15

CHAPTER 1 19
Following Jesus: A Ticket Outta Hell
or Something Much More?

CHAPTER 2 33
Cherry-Picking the Scriptures, New Testament-Style

CHAPTER 3 53
The Bible: Rated R for Graphic Divine Violence,
Disturbing Images, and Strong Language

CHAPTER 4 67
Marcionite! An In-vogue Strawman

CHAPTER 5 75
God made Adam, Eve, *and* Steve

CHAPTER 6 87
Indeed Very Many: Universalism in the Early Church

CHAPTER 7 97
The Cross of Christ: Pulling a Sacrificial One-Eighty

CHAPTER 8 113
Locked from the Inside? Predestination,
Free Will, and the Doctrine of Hell

CHAPTER 9 131
The Wrath (of God): Revealed from
Heaven or from the Human Heart?

CHAPTER 10 143
Kickin' Ass and Takin' Names

APPENDIX A 159
Many Voices, One Message

APPENDIX B 165
Could It Be...*the* Satan?

APPENDIX C 173
Paul's Universalism: A Brief Exegesis of Romans 5:12–19,
1 Corinthians 15:22–28, and Colossians 1:15–20

APPENDIX D 181
Universal Reconciliation: A Compilation
of New Testament Passages

END NOTES 187

BIBLIOGRAPHY 199

Foreword

Music will always have a special place in my heart. As a child, I can recall how special it was anytime someone complemented me on my ability to sing along with what I heard on the radio. I understood melody, harmony, and timing; the three essentials to a quality tune. But I understood when and how to be creative as well, when to add something outside the written music. As I grew up, my life only became more infused with the sweet sound of song. To that end, I became involved in competitive choirs all throughout high school, sang in multiple worship teams, and was even a part of the creation of a worship album.

Now, when I was younger, I attended a church with my grandmother and have vivid memories of sitting in a pew, listening to the chorus of voices around me. I often felt some sense of embarrassment because my grandmother was always out of key. And more than that, she always sang louder than I thought was necessary. Compared to those around us, she stuck out like a sore thumb. Yet, she never seemed to mind. No one else did either. But, I was painfully aware and even felt that it reflected badly on me. Such is the narcissistic nature of a young child (as if adults are any better.) It never registered in my mind that she seemed so happy and comfortable in her worship.

You may be wondering what it is about these specific memories of discomfort that have stayed with me, and, to be honest, for the longest time, I simply did not know. It was only recently that they began to make sense.

You see, my life has, in so many ways, resembled my time in those pews. Like sitting next to my out-of-tune grandmother, it has been wrought with discomfort—my belief systems painfully turned upside down with one thought that began to roll like a boulder down a steep hill. I could not stop the progress and I could not go back to what I previously "knew," no matter how much I wanted to. I was stuck dealing with the changes and after a while, just went with it, even when it produced feelings of anxiety and panic. That sounds dramatic, but it is accurate; there certainly were days in which I could not sit still, where all my thoughts led to an uncomfortable disquieting in my soul. Probably the most difficult experience during this time was the lack of those with whom I could commiserate. In fact, my doctrinal questioning eventually resulted in me being asked to walk away from my church home completely.

Shortly after meeting Matthew—around the time he released his first book—I, in keeping with my new-found habit of stepping outside my comfort zone, traveled to his release party and met a new group of friends face-to-face that were all questioning the same things as me. Consequently, after I read *All Set Free*, I was forced to consider yet more question-inducing material. As the questions began to pile up, the pressure was definitely on. When the answers alluded me, things only got worse. Nevertheless, what I discovered is that questions are the best part of life, and, in the uncertainty, faith is actually found. I had always considered faith as being certain of something, but upon further reflection—and countless conversations—I have found it's actually the opposite.

So, back to my musical memories…

One thing I learned as I worked with vocal instructors is that the melody is the driving force in any song. Without a strong melody, the harmonies will always sound wrong. However, when put together in the correct way, the collaboration brings about wonderful tunes that appeal on many different levels. The same is true as it applies to wrestling with the questions that arise from our belief systems. While we can apply the basic tenets of Christianity to the idea of a melody—the Apostles' or Nicene Creed, for example—it is the wrestling with the tough questions that adds the harmony, bringing the whole song together.

Far too often, however, the tough questions are treated as dissonant noise that must be stamped out in the name of "core beliefs." Yet, as I've learned, in all reality it's our supposed "core beliefs" that are the cause of all the dissonance. Questioning things has shown me this.

In this book, Matthew dares to question a number of subjects that are considered taboo within the Church at-large. Questions such as the existence of hell—or lack thereof—Universalism, homosexuality, and others, are sure to make a few people squirm in their seats. But, these are the very questions that would not leave me alone and produced in me the panic at finding myself in the uncomfortable position of having to change my mind. To that end, it is my personal opinion that the questions explored in these chapters are necessary, if the Church is to truly take its place as the bride of Christ, constantly reforming toward his image and likeness.

—MICHELLE COLLINS

Preface

Am I a heretic? The title of this book seems to suggest so. However, I'll let you in on a little secret: I'm really not. I may be cheeky, and I'm certainly crass, but I'm not a heretic. That is, not according to either the Apostles' or Nicene creeds. And the last I checked, these were the standards for what is and is not considered heretical in Christianity. At least, they were supposed to be.

So, if I'm not really a heretic, why call this book "Heretic!?" Well, it's simple: I've been labelled a "heretic" so many fucking times, I thought "What the hell? Why not wear it as an ironic badge of honor?" It's sort of like how the 2004 Boston Red Sox, in spite of how great a team they were, called themselves "the idiots." Why? Because that's sort of what they looked like: a bunch of "idiots" with long hair and beards, strong personalities, and lots and lots of flair. And in a game like baseball, where there are supposed to be certain rules to abide by—think of how the New York Yankees do business—that kind of stuff just ain't gonna fly. Christian theology, at least here in the United States, is sort of like that. Only instead of being called "idiots," those who don't quite fit the mold are called "heretics," "false prophets," "reprobates," and all sorts of other harmfully judgmental things.

All of this certainly raises the question: If I'm not technically a heretic, why *does* such a label get branded onto me so very often? Well, I honestly don't think most Christians actually know the difference between orthodoxy, heterodoxy, and heresy. So, when certain Christians come across my theology, they just brand it heretical because it doesn't line up with theirs. Simply put, my theology doesn't include eternal torment (*Heresy!*), penal substitutionary atonement theory (*Heresy!*), biblical inerrancy (*Heresy!*), the Rapture (*Heresy!*), divine violence (*Heresy!*), exclusion of the LGBTQ+ community (*Heresy!*), and much more (*HERESY!*). However, as we'll hopefully discover throughout this book, none of these issues are actually heretical; not in formal terms anyway. They may be unpopular, but so what? The last I checked, truth doesn't give a shit about how many people believe it or not. Truth is truth, and has nothing to do with popularity.

So, to all the idiotic heretics out there, here's to you! Cheers, and enjoy the book.

Acknowledgments

Where would I be without my wife Lyndsay? I dare not imagine. So, I must first and foremost thank her for being my rock. And to her mini-me, our daughter Elyse, who always finds a way to bring a smile to my face: Thank you, my sweet princess.

My closest friend is Michael Machuga, and I owe him a huge debt of gratitude for the way he has impacted my life. Mike is, without a doubt, the Gimli to my Legolas—sans the bright red beard.

My parents, Dave and Sharon, have always been dedicated mentors and lifelong friends. I am quite thankful for the wise council I've received throughout the years.

I have to give a shout-out to my fellow heretics from the Heretic Happy Hour podcast. Keith Giles, Jamal Jivanjee, and Rafael Polendo, you guys are the fucking best. Let's keep this train a-rollin'.

I'm grateful to those who have read the manuscript and offered their thoughts and critique, and especially to Mark Hilditch for offering his editing services. Thanks also to the focus group who provided valuable feedback: Rob Edwards, Nathan Jennings, Bryan Johnson, Dietrich Lange, Juanita Ponce, and Simone Ramacci.

A hearty "thank you" to everyone who provided the lovely quotes that were used on the back cover of this book. Without your uplifting words of wisdom, I couldn't have found quite the same motivation.

And to everyone that I've failed to mention, *thank you*. Truly. I haven't the room to name you all, but you know who you are, and you haven't gone unnoticed. I couldn't do what I do without all the support I receive from each and every one of you.

Namaste.

Introduction

I have been "doing theology" publicly—on Facebook and elsewhere—for roughly four years. If you've engaged with me on that platform then you know it has been quite an interesting ride to say the least. If you have not, then what you must know about me is that I rarely, if ever, sugarcoat things. I don't pull punches and I don't let harmful ideas go unnoticed. Furthermore, I put a lot—I mean *a lot*—of ideas out there, and try to remain as transparent as possible. This can lead to some fun banter, but it is not without its risks. Sometimes it bites me in the ass and I am forced to publicly admit where I have been in error. The ego is not a fan of such things. Yet, ultimately, this is a good thing as we all must grow, and how can we do so unless we challenge ourselves and our current beliefs? Given this reality, then, sometimes you just have to take it on the chin and learn from your mistakes.

Being an author and theologian who affirms universal reconciliation, and who is, to some extent, currently positioned in the public eye, I have been afforded the opportunity to be asked a litany of thought-provoking questions. Because of this, I've gotten a feel as to what is on people's minds. Indeed, while some questions have been absolutely dreadful—hostile, angry, purely emotional, and on a few occasions, even laden with physical threats—others have forced me to push myself and grow in ways I never thought imaginable.

It is these we will focus on throughout the book.

If I may be so bold, the thought of universal salvation, at least initially, evokes a visceral response from most Evangelicals that goes something like this: "Well if *that* is the case, then what is the point in following Jesus?!" Because I have been asked this question so many times, I thought it best to tackle it right off the bat in chapter 1. Then, in chapter 2, we'll address the subject of biblical cherry-picking. It seems this is an issue with scores of Protestants, who tend to believe that if you do not affirm every theological claim in the Bible then you are just flippantly picking whichever cherries you desire. This couldn't be further from the truth, as rather than being frivolous cherry pickers we will in fact be following Jesus of Nazareth and the Apostle Paul as our models in how to read the Scriptures.

Chapter 3 will build upon chapter 2. We'll touch on René Girard's mimetic theory and explain why, throughout history, regardless of culture or religion, qualities like vengeance and a desire for sacrifice are so quickly and consistently *projected* onto the divine. Then, piggybacking off this, chapter 4 will explore why our understanding of the Scriptures is different than what is known as Marcionism—an unfair charge that has often been levied against Girardians such as myself, or pretty much anyone else who says that *God's nature is exactly like Jesus'*.

Chapter 5 will cover the issue of homosexuality, which can be a most contentious subject. But, we will not shy away as we attempt to put forth an argument for the full inclusion of the GSM (Gender and Sexual Minority) community into the Church at-large.

Chapter 6 will explore Universalist thought in the early Church, as it seems we tend to forget just how acceptable a doctrine it was for many Patristic Fathers.

Chapter 7 will address the charge that I've abandoned the cross, which really means that I've abandoned the penal substitutionary theory of the atonement (which I gladly admit to doing). Yet, as we shall see, I'm hardly the first to think of the cross in a non-penal way.

In chapter 8, we will move on to the topic of free will. Most Christians contend one of two things: that scores of human beings will ultimately be lost to the flames of hell on account of their own "freedom," or that God sends them there. Nevertheless, as we'll hopefully discover, both views have their major pitfalls.

Chapter 9 will then deal with the notion that God's love and wrath are somehow mutually exclusive, juxtaposed against one another, rather than God's wrath, like all other attributes, being that which flows from his infinite outpouring of love.

Finally, our closing chapter will be a discussion about a topic that used to scare the living daylights out of me, namely, the End Times™ and more specifically, the less than two-hundred-year-old doctrine known as the Rapture.

Now, all that being said, please do not think of this book as some end-all-be-all when it comes to theological matters. It is far from *that*! Rather, it is a simple and succinct set of answers to the questions I hear most often. Perhaps we can even call it my confession of faith, where I opt for brevity more often than not. Forgive me (there's a lengthy bibliography if you desire to dig deeper). Nevertheless, if you do not find yourself in agreement with me, then that is perfectly fine (as if you need my approval!) Maybe you can write a letter if you see fit. I am always open to dialoguing about these issues, so long as things stay respectful and kind. Theological discourse constantly excites me; a vigorous debate is something to be cherished, rather than feared and shied away from. Just don't call me a heretic or worse—not unless you want to end up on the back cover of a book. ☺

Take from this book what you will. I do my best to keep things short and to the point. Often times I am cheeky, and sometimes I can be rather biting. I hope that is okay with you. Oh, and I cuss from time to time.

So, bear with me...

In spite of these rough edges, however, the heart of this project is love. Love is the reason I do what I do and, in fact, is the reason why any of us exist in the first place. So, my goal is to spread love and to proclaim, in the words of my wife's favorite author, Rob Bell, that love wins! All else is just the particulars, which this book attempts to decipher. Perhaps I am off a bit, but aren't we all? Yet, in spite of such error, as Bernard Ramm teaches: "God forgives our theology...just like he forgives our sin."[1]

Thank God for that!

1
Following Jesus: A Ticket Outta Hell or Something Much More?

"Whenever universalism is espoused, the urgency and energy of the New Testament preaching is dissipated. I tell you, it is a very unusual thing to hear a Barthian say, 'I beseech you, be reconciled to God.' And it is an even rarer thing to hear a card-carrying, genuine-article universalist publicly espousing the doctrine of universalism with tears in his eyes, to say, 'I beg you; lay down your arms; be reconciled to God.'"[1]

—JOHN PIPER

"If universalism is true…it is not necessary to preach the gospel at all, since everyone is already on their way to God and heaven, whether or not they have the Son."[2]

—ALEXANDER M. JORDAN

I'm not being hyperbolic when I say that questions like "If all are saved, then why follow Jesus?" are my least favorite variety, and for a litany of reasons. Primarily, it is because questions like these seem to assume that if there is no eternal hell awaiting us should we fail to choose Jesus as "personal lord and savior" in this life, then Jesus is not worth following. As if Jesus doesn't stand on his own. As if our primary concern as Christians should be the afterlife, rather than ushering in the *at-hand* kingdom of heaven. As if the Way of Jesus comes down to an acknowledgement that he is who he says he is, merely some secret password St. Peter requires prior to letting us in through the Pearly Gates, rather than a way of discipleship directly handed to us from the Master and the first apostles. But, is the former the thrust of the New Testament? Should hell-avoidance be our primary concern? Let's take a look, shall we?

Point 1: The Gospel Brings Peace, *Now*

"As shoes for your feet put on whatever will make you ready to proclaim the gospel of peace."

—EPHESIANS 6:15

"And the peace of God, which transcends all understanding, will guard your hearts and your minds in Christ Jesus."

—PHILIPPIANS 4:7

In case you haven't noticed, our world is, and has always been, a violent one. The history books prove this. The present moment proves this. Just look around you. Syria is a mess. Palestine is in shambles—so too is Afghanistan, Iraq, Turkey, Yemen, Libya, Somalia, Ethiopia, Honduras, Brazil, Mexico, and on and on. This unfortunate reality also includes my country, the United States of America. Recently, the *always-on-the-brink-of-war* US—by the way, a "Christian" nation, as I'm often told—just chose for its President a "Christian" man whose solution to defeat terrorism is, in part, to "take out their families,"[3] over a "Christian" woman notorious for her pro-war voting record and dubious—dare I say *un-Christlike*—political dealings. It seems that, in one way or another, this perpetual war we find ourselves in will muster up a way to continue on *ad infinitum*.

Then, on top of our precarious sociopolitical situation, our city streets are witnessing increased mimetic aggression, both from and toward police, and *random* acts of violence, while statistically trending downward, are still flooding the scene. Furthermore, Mother Earth is taking a beating: deforestation, increased severe weather patterns, the Pacific garbage patch, the Fukushima incident, the depopulation of the bees, and so on. It is overwhelmingly apparent, then, that violence—including violence toward our planet—is quickly getting out of control and at some point, we will have to face a reaping of what we are currently sowing. The worst-case scenario, of course, is that we may just one day find ourselves booted off our tiny blue dot, either because of nuclear destruction, a piling up of ecological disasters, and/or for any number of other reasons too numerous to list. Think of it as a global Gehenna of sorts.[4]

I do not say these things to sound like an alarmist. Ultimately, I remain an optimist. Yet, I also realize the reality of our plight. It's not beyond the realm of possibilities for humanity to enter into an all-out nuclear war at some point, not when our planet has something to the tune of 15,500 total nukes (as of August, 2016[5]). And, if any of the nine nations that possess these weapons start going all red button on us, then it's probably game over—unless you want to live underground for the rest of your life. I don't.

So, here's the rub: Given what could be considered some pretty gloomy prognostications, do we not need "saving" from a very real "something?" And is that something not violence? Has it not always been about violence? Isn't the Gospel relevant when thinking about the real crisis humanity finds herself in, and, in fact, has seemingly always found herself in?

You bet it is!

This is what the Gospel has been about from the start: A breaking into our time and space by God to show humanity what true humanness, as well as perfect theology, is all about. And all of it—I mean *all* of it—is centered on God's liberating grace and perpetual love. Only now, this beautifully good news has been hijacked and made out to be nothing more than securing for ourselves some blissful afterlife—at the expense of those who burn for all eternity—rather than ushering in the peaceful kingdom of heaven in the *here* and *now*. But, the latter is exactly what we need to get back to because at its core, the Gospel has never so much been about posthumous rewards, or being saved from the Father—may it never be that—but about liberation from our enslavement to the violent powers and principalities that structure our out-of-shape world.

One of these foundational mechanisms is called *scapegoating*. We see this culture-structuring principle on full display in the Passion narrative, for example, when the High Priest Caiaphas proclaims: "It is better for you to have *one man die for the people* than to have the whole nation destroyed" (John 11:50, emphasis mine). You see, this is just how scapegoating works, how it leads to (false) peace. When a community is in crisis, they sacrifice one *for* the rest. This is emphasized by Luke's Gospel, when the writer notices how former rivals—Pilate and Herod—unite around the death of Jesus: "That *same day* Herod and Pilate became friends with each other; *before this they had been enemies.*" (Luke 23:12, emphasis mine)

The Passion exposes this wicked truth about humanity, though, and then offers a way out. That Way is the Way of Forgiveness, even in the face of the violent mechanisms that make up human culture. Jesus models this in Luke 23:34 when, naked from the cross, he continually cries out "Father, forgive them; for they do not know what they are doing."[6] Here, Jesus speaks to the nonconscious nature of what is driving this event—*they do not know what they are doing*—and then unveils, for all to see, how to end this cycle of violence. It will be through forgiveness, and by not counting their sins against them (2 Cor 5:19; cf. Jer 31:34); and it will be out in the open—*outside the city gate in order to sanctify the people by his own blood* (Heb 13:12)—rather than in the Temple, behind the veil, where sacrifices were generally made.[7]

This Way that Jesus opens up for us is how "thy kingdom come" manifests itself on earth "as it is in heaven" (Matt 6:10). From Jesus, we learn that in spite of our human kingdoms being structured with retributive violence to the extent of seventy-sevenfold—as when Lamech boasts of murdering a child for merely scratching him (Gen 4:24)—the kingdom of God is established by forgiveness offered to one another seventy-sevenfold (Matt 18:22). The crescendo of this message is the Passion and Resurrection.

Indeed, the Resurrection picks up where the Passion leaves off. Actually, it does more than that. It unveils the slain yet forgiving victim, whose blood speaks a *better* word than the blood of Abel (Heb 12:24). In Genesis 4:10, Abel's blood cries for vengeance. But Jesus, both from the cross and then after it, cries for forgiveness and peace. And when he does this, others (like you and I) have the ability to taste, see, and trust in his Way even unto death, because in the end, all is forgiven and all will be made alive again—on what the writer of Acts calls the "time of the restoration of all things" (Acts 3:21). In the meantime, though, our calling as Christians, or in other words our "election," is to follow in this path of peace that our Master set before us, pleading with others to be "reconciled to God"—*here* and *now*.

Point 2: Death Looms— Watching, Waiting

"So that through death he might destroy the one who has the power of death, that is, the devil, and free those who all their lives were held in slavery by the fear of death."

—HEB 2:14-15

All of us, in one way or another, are destined to die; whether by some horrific event early on in life or simply from a wearing down of the bodies we are currently riding around in, it's inevitable. Frankly, this scares the living shit out of us. Pulitzer Prize winning anthropologist Ernest Becker even posited that our fear of death is the *primary* driving force behind humanity's gruesome violence (more on that in chapter 7).[8] And to a great extent, I tend to agree with him.

You see, while human beings are unique in our ability to create symbols—language, works of art, of music, and of poetry—along with this beautiful gift comes the ability to also think symbolically about our future death. So, in addition to carrying with us the type of anxiety all animals possess (i.e., "fight or flight"), we also develop an anxiety of the more neurotic variety. When we do this, we create entire systems—religions, cultures, etc.—to protect our idea of the "immortal self." The major problem, then, is that these systems tend to crash into other systems, causing hostility and conflict that can last for ages (just ask anyone who has been caught up in the Palestinian/Israeli conflict).

But, there is a *Christocentric* (Christ-centered) solution to this problem, one that is driven home, not only by the writer of Hebrews, but also by the Apostle Paul in Romans 5. Here's a very quick run-down of what Paul has to say about the issue of death in vv. 12–19 of that chapter:

> In v.12, Paul tells us that Adam's sin leads to *death* for *all* people. Then in v.14 he writes how death even exercises *dominion* over us (cf. 1 Cor 15:56; Heb 2:14–15). That is to say, death and the fear it causes, holds humanity in bondage, making it completely juxtaposed against the life-giving gift Christ freely gives (Rom 5:17–18, 21). To that end, for Paul, what Adam did, Christ undid—Adam's sin undone by Christ's free gift of grace, universal death in Adam *undone* by universal life in a crucified yet raised Christ.

Paul is so confident of this that in his first letter to the Corinthians, he describes *death* as being "swallowed up in victory" (1 Cor 15:54). One verse later, he even mocks death itself: "Where, O death, is your victory? Where, O death, is your sting?" (1 Cor 15:55; cf. Hos 13:14)

A bold proclamation, don't ya think!

The early Christians, Paul included, were bold people though. They took all sorts of unjust abuse because of their faith. They were accused of cannibalism (due to their eucharistic practices), accused of atheism[9] (they would not bow to the Romans gods), scapegoated for a tragic fire that tore through first century Rome,[10] and butchered by the thousands. During Nero's reign, their burning bodies were even used to light up the night sky.[11] Yet, they remained true to Christ, their Master. They were always forgiving, even going so far as to open their homes to one another, living wholly *for* the "other." One could say they lived as if they had already died with Christ (Col 3:3). But, because Christ had been raised, so were they.

O, death, where is thy sting, indeed!

To that end, what I want to emphasize to those who, doctrinally, need an eternal hell in order to follow Jesus is this: *Death* and our *fear of death* is enough of a hell to be saved from. The early Christians recognized this, which is why the theme of death and Christ's victory over it—and not over an eternal torture chamber called hell—is so prevalent in the Christus Victor model of the atonement (which we'll discuss in chapter 7). Nevertheless, it's a model that makes intuitive sense, ringing true in my heart of hearts, because it means that there is a *real* saving from something—that is, from death and our fear of it—not a speculative saving from a speculative hellacious afterlife.

Point 3: Jesus Asks Us To

This is the most "duh-worthy" answer of the three. No matter what we believe about eschatology, soteriology, or any of the other "-ologies," doesn't Jesus—the incarnate Word (Logos[12]) of God—ask us to follow him, *full stop?* To put it another way, isn't our theology subservient to our Jesus-following, and not the other way around? The Bible—which, incidentally, is not the Word (Logos) of God—is fairly clear about this: (All emphasis mine)

- Matthew 4:19: "And he said to them, '*Follow me*, and I will make you fish for people.'"

- Matthew 16:24: "Then Jesus said to his disciples, 'Whoever wants to be my disciple must deny themselves and take up their cross and *follow me*.'"

- Matthew 19:28: "Jesus said to them, 'Truly I tell you, at the renewal of all things, when the Son of Man sits on his glorious throne, you who have *followed me* will also sit on the twelve thrones, judging the twelve tribes of Israel.'"

- Mark 10:21: "Jesus, looking at him, loved him and said, 'You lack one thing; go, sell what you own, and give the money to the poor, and you will have treasure in heaven; then come, *follow me*.'"

- John 8:12: "Again Jesus spoke to them, saying, 'I am the light of the world. Whoever *follows me* will never walk in darkness but will have the light of life.'"

- John 21:18–19: "'Very truly, I tell you, when you were younger you used to fasten your own belt and to go wherever you wished. But when you grow old, you will stretch out your hands, and someone else will fasten a belt around you and take you where you do not wish to go.' (He said this to indicate the kind of death by which he would glorify God.) After this he said to him, '*Follow me*.'"

This call to follow Jesus is not some arbitrary command, however, but something much, much more. You see, given humanity's copycat nature, we are going to follow someone, and generally non-consciously. And the fact of the matter is that this will generally lead to rivalries and violence; for you see, because we all want what the other has, and because we all cannot have it, it becomes simple mathematics.

Think of the opening scene from *Lord of the Rings: The Return of the King*. Two friends, Sméagol and Déagol, are fishing in a river, when Déagol gets dragged down by a lunker. While under the water, he discovers the infamous Ring. Once at the surface, Sméagol arrives and then picks up on Déagol's deep desire for the ring. Sure enough, the two then get into a knock-down-drag-out fight in which Sméagol slays Déagol. And that, my friends, is basically what we humans do to each other any time something *shiny* comes our way. We just cannot help ourselves. Our desires become so twisted that we often lose our humanity and will stop at nothing to acquire these desires. We'll even slay our own brother or sister if we have to.

Here, Tolkien absolutely hits the nail on the head!

But, the Hebrew Bible also speaks to this in its founding murder myth. Cain slays Abel because he desires what he believes Abel has, namely God's blessing (Gen 4:3–5). The rivalry that is fueled by the brothers' shared desires brings a lurking of sin to Cain's door (Gen 4:7).[13] Cain then lets sin enter one verse later, when brother rises up against brother, spilling the first human blood. The Bible speaks truth to power here, soberly yet accurately depicting how all of human culture is founded on blood.

So, thinking again about Jesus…

Jesus refuses to enter into these sorts of rivalries with others. He does not do this simply because he is God—that is, a being with superhuman abilities (i.e., Docetism)—but because he, as the True Human, intimately knows the Father's heart. On numerous occasions, the writer of John's Gospel gives an account of the bond between the Son and the Father:

- John 5:19–20: "The Son can do nothing on his own, but only what he sees the Father doing; for whatever the Father does, the Son does likewise."

- John 6:38: "For I have come down from heaven, not to do my own will, but the will of him who sent me."

- John 8:28: "I do nothing on my own, but I speak these things as the Father instructed me."

- John 10:29: "What my Father has given me is greater than all else, and no one can snatch it out of the Father's hand."

- John 12:49: "For I have not spoken on my own, but the Father who sent me has himself given me a commandment about what to say and what to speak."

Now, as we began exploring in section 1, what Jesus Christ reveals about the divine is that divinity possesses no violence. God is a life-giver—*only*. Reality is structured, not by violence, but by love, which is also to say mercy (Matt 5:38; Luke 6:36). In fact, God is love itself (1 John 4:18). He is also light and in him there is no darkness (1 John 1:5). This includes the darkness of imitative rivalry, the very darkness that plagues humanity and drives us to such retributive violence.

> What Jesus Christ reveals about the divine is that divinity possesses no violence. God is a life-giver—*only*.

That darkness is purely a human thing!

In Matthew 16:21–23, we witness it quite clearly in the back and forth between Jesus and Peter. Notice how, after Jesus foretells of his own death, Peter attempts to persuade Jesus to do contrary to what the Father was having him do. It is as if Peter is saying "no" to following Jesus, instead desiring Jesus to follow him. French anthropologist René Girard offers great insight into how a rivalry could have been born during this event:

> Instead of imitating Jesus, Peter wants Jesus to imitate him. If two friends imitate each other's desires, they both desire the same object. And if they cannot share this object, they will compete for it, each becoming simultaneously a model and an obstacle to each other. The competing desires intensify as model and obstacle reinforce each other, and an escalation of mimetic rivalry follows; admiration gives way to indignation, jealousy, envy, hatred, and, at last, violence and vengeance. Had Jesus imitated Peter's ambition, the two thereby would have begun competing for the leadership of some politicized "Jesus

movement." Sensing the danger, Jesus vehemently interrupts Peter: "Get behind me, Satan, you are a skandalon to me."[14]

Jesus understands the temptation of taking on a model other than the Father (Luke 4:1–11). He understands how enticing the satan can be and recognizes it as *skandalon*, or a stumbling block. In *this* case, it is Peter's desire to have Jesus follow him that is the skandalon personified—"Satan." If Jesus would have followed Peter, the nonviolent Christ-mission would have failed and the two would have entered into a rivalrous situation, one that would have potentially escalated toward overt violence, either among Jesus and Peter and the disciples, or with those in Jerusalem where Jesus would soon be going, or both.

> Because we simply cannot turn off our desires, we instead must imitate the desires of a figure that only does the will of the non-rivalrous Father. That figure is Christ Jesus.

This is why following Jesus is so important. Because we simply cannot turn off our desires, we instead must imitate the desires of a figure that only does the will of the non-rivalrous Father. That figure is Christ Jesus. It is he who can lead us, en masse, into the kingdom of heaven. It is he who best exposes humanity's propensity toward rivalry, and then he who models how to replace that with positive imitation—i.e., non-consciousness replaced by a higher consciousness.

It may not be a simple task, but it is the Christian calling—or again, our "election." And because this way of life is not an easy one, crosses must be carried daily (Luke 9:23), as it remains a daily struggle for most people, including myself. Yet, since Jesus asked this of us, and then showed us exactly how to do it, it is exactly what we, as *Christ*-ians, should do. Not because we have to, or because if we do then we can "go to heaven when we die," but simply because that is what Jesus asked of us.

2
Cherry-Picking the Scriptures, New Testament-Style

"[Christian] Liberalism leads away from biblical fidelity and compromises scriptural truth. It only needs the door to be open a crack in order to push its way through. The only guarantee against the liberal influence on the church is to set our minds and eyes upon the word of God, study it diligently, and believe what it says."[1]

—MATT SLICK

"Progressive Christians despise God's word when it comes to hating sin. They will only talk about God's love and watch the hate they spew once they find you don't support their beliefs. But remember God's warnings regarding false teachers (2 Tim 4:2–4) and differing gospels."[2]

—CARLOTTA MORROW

Am I a biblical cherry picker? *Yes, actually, that is pretty much what I am.* Do you want to know why? (And no, it is not because I despise God's "word.") It is because that is pretty much what both Jesus and Paul were (ducks and covers). But, seriously, they were. Well, they did not have Bibles per se, but you know what I mean—they "cherry-picked" their Scriptures. Yet, it's not enough to simply leave it at that, because their cherry-picking was in a strikingly consistent manner; where certain theological claims that were embedded into Second Temple Jewish thought—most notably, that God is, among other things, a vengeful and cursing God—are eliminated. That is simply to say, they had a "nonviolent hermeneutic." Now, so you do not think I'm bat-shit-crazy for saying this, let's explore some of these instances. (It will help you to have a Bible handy for the rest of this chapter.)

Jesus

INSTANCE 1: LUKE 4:16-30, REFERENCING ISAIAH 61:1-2

Allow me to set the scene. We begin in Luke 3, where Jesus is baptized by John the Baptist. Filled with the Holy Spirit, Jesus then heads out into the wilderness (Luke 4:1). Here, he is tested by the devil. But, like a Kung Fu master, Jesus dismisses the satan, passing the ultimate test. While in the power of the Spirit, Jesus then heads to the synagogue in Nazareth to proclaim the jubilant good news that he is about to bring. When he arrives, he opens the scroll of the prophet Isaiah, turning right to the Jubilee text from chapter 61 (one of everyone's favorites), and reads:

"The Spirit of the Lord is upon me,
  Because he has anointed me
    To bring good news to the poor.
  He has sent me to proclaim release to the captives
    And recovery of sight to the blind,

>To let the oppressed go free,
>To proclaim the year of the Lord's favor."
>
>—Luke 4:18–19

Rolling up the scroll, Jesus makes a full stop, midsentence, and boldly proclaims, "Today this scripture has been fulfilled in your hearing" (Luke 4:21). Then, in the very next verse, *you-know-what* hits the fan. And before you retort by saying "that's not what the next verse says," let me clarify something.

In Luke 4:22, the passage in most biblical translations indeed reads "all spoke well of him," but in all reality, the Greek text simply says πάντες ἐμαρτύρουν αὐτῷ, or "all bore witness to him."[3] So what is going on here? Scholar Michael Hardin, in his masterful work *The Jesus Driven Life*, offers a compelling answer:

> Translators have to make what is known as a syntactical decision, they have to decide whether or not the "bearing witness" is negative or positive. Technically speaking they have to decide if the dative pronoun "to him" is a dative of disadvantage or a dative of advantage; was the crowd bearing witness to his advantage or to his disadvantage?[4]

In other words, translators have to make a choice: Was the crowd enthralled with Jesus' message, bearing positive witness, and proud that Jesus was Joseph's son? Or, rather, were they upset by it, and bore negative witness to it by dismissing Jesus as the son of a "nobody?" (After all, as John 1:46 teaches, nothing good ever came out of Nazareth). Well, it seems that based on Jesus' sarcastic response in vv. 23–27 that the latter is more accurate. Otherwise, why would he get defensive for seemingly no reason? It is doubtful he would. Instead, it seems more reasonable to think that Jesus is responding to the jeering crowd in front of him. The reverse makes little sense.

But, a key question remains: *Why* were they so pissed off to begin with? What gets them all riled up in the first place? The answer, to put it plainly, is in how Jesus reads the text from Isaiah. Notice, in Isaiah 61:2, a key feature to the Jubilee passage is "the day of vengeance of our God." But Jesus does not read this part. In fact, he stops midsentence in order to omit the theological claim that God was going to bring vengeance down upon the very people he, as well as the prophets Elijah and Elisha before him, were sent by God to bless. For Jesus, unlike his interlocutors, God was *not* going to deliver his people from Roman occupation through the use of vengeance; instead, he was going to bring good news to *all* the poor, proclaim release to *all* the captives, recovery of sight to *all* the blind; he was going to let *all* the oppressed go free, and proclaim the year of the Lord's favor without any such eschatological violence.

This is what gets the crowd in a tizzy. And that is why they then "bear witness" to Jesus, not advantageously, but disadvantageously. They are upset over Jesus' omission of a very key part of the Isaianic text, which leads them to sarcastically dismiss Jesus as merely "the son of Joseph," or in other words, the son of a "nobody" (cf. John 1:46). Hence Jesus' retort: "No prophet is accepted in the prophet's hometown" (Luke 4:24).

To sum all this up: What the people cannot accept here is a teacher who teaches that a Day of Jubilee is a day *without* "the vengeance of our God" (Isa 61:2). It is such an offensive claim, in fact, that they nearly throw Jesus off a cliff because of it (Luke 4:29–30). Indeed, Jesus must have learned, that very day, just how dangerous it is to mess with folks' presupposed doctrines.

INSTANCE 2: LUKE 7:18-23, REFERENCING VARIOUS PASSAGES FROM ISAIAH; 1 AND 2 KINGS

Here's our second scene. John the Baptist is in a bit of a pickle. He really wants to know if Jesus is the messiah, "the one who is to come" (Luke 7:20). But, he is also in prison for speaking out against King Herod and his minions. So, to solve this conundrum, John sends some of his disciples to speak with Jesus in order to clarify just who Jesus really is. However, when John's disciples reach Jesus and ask John's questions, Jesus, in typical Jesus fashion, does not simply answer *yes* or *no*, but instead offers a multilayered and highly technical response.

The answer Jesus provides primarily consists of scriptural quotations from Isaiah (and some from First and Second Kings). He informs the disciples to tell John that the blind receive sight (Isa 29:18; 35:5; 61:1–2), the lame walk (Isa 35:6), the lepers are cleansed (2 Kgs 5:1–27), the deaf hear (Isa 29:18; 35:5), the dead are raised (1 Kgs 17:17–34), and the poor have good news brought to them (Isa 29:19). Like the story from Luke 4, though, there is something going on under the surface that we must pay attention to.

You see, John the Baptist most likely shared a similar eschatology with the folks in Nazareth—the ones who were ready to throw Jesus from a cliff for his elimination of "the day of vengeance of our God" from Second Isaiah. We see evidence of this in Luke 3:7–9, where John warns the people of "the wrath to come."⁵ So, it's quite telling that when Jesus quotes the above Isaianic passages, he *always* eliminates the associated vengeance texts.

See for yourself. Isaiah 29:18 and 29:19 are referenced, but not Isaiah 29:20: "~~For the tyrant shall be no more, and the scoffer shall cease to be; all those alert to do evil shall be cut off~~"; Isaiah 35:5 and 35:6 are included, but not Isaiah 35:4: "~~Here is your God. He will come with vengeance, with terrible recompense~~"; and Isaiah 61:1–2 is used, but not the phrase "and the day of vengeance of our God" from v. 2.⁶ Then, Jesus does a mic drop, when he concludes with: "And blessed is anyone who takes no offense at me" (Luke 7:23). The offense he is talking about here is the same offense caused in the synagogue in Nazareth. It is the offense, or scandal, of a non-vengeful Father. But, for those who are not offended, they will find blessing here, because they will see that God indeed blesses everyone. That is the exact message Jesus gives in Matthew 5:45, when he teaches that God "sends rain on the righteous and on the unrighteous"—which, by the way, is a direct subversion of the very Deuteronomic God Jesus' contemporaries so often affirmed, the God who were told will "change the rain of your land into powder, and only dust shall come down upon you from the sky until you are destroyed." (Deut 28:24)

INSTANCE 3: MATTHEW 5, REFERENCING LEVITICUS 24:20; VARIOUS PASSAGES FROM DEUTERONOMY 28

Scene three: The Sermon on the Mount. Here, Jesus makes some very interesting statements that should garner our attention. On a number of occasions, he begins a teaching with "You have heard that it was said, but I say to you." What this means is that he is going to be quoting from his Scriptures, and then follow that with a fresh take on how to apply the instructions. So, for instance, contrary to Leviticus 24:20, in Matthew 5:38–39, Jesus says "You have heard that it was said, 'An eye for an eye and a tooth for a tooth,' but I say to you, Do not resist an evildoer. But, if anyone strikes you on the right cheek, turn the other also." However, Jesus also qualifies these teachings with the statement: "Do not think that I have come to abolish the law or the prophets; I have not come to abolish, but to fulfill" (Matt 5:17).

So, what is going on here?

> Jesus is not necessarily affirming the letter of every law, but the spirit behind the whole of it.

First off, we have to figure out if by "fulfill" Jesus meant that he came to affirm *every jot and tittle* in the whole of the "law and prophets," or that he came to perfect and complete them. This is to ask, is Jesus simply agreeing with all the teachings of Moses and the other Hebrew writers, or is he the *telos*, or ultimate goal, of them? To address this, we should simply ask ourselves this: how did Jesus interpret the passages he quotes?

Well, given his direct "contradiction"—or, rather, expansion—of multiple teachings (namely those from Lev 24:20; Deut 28:15, 20–24, 59–61; Eccles 5:4), we should conclude the latter; that Jesus is not necessarily affirming the letter of every law, but the spirit behind the whole of it. In other words, when we say that Jesus fulfills the Law, what we're not saying is that every theological datum in the whole of the Law and prophets must be affirmed, but that the *whole* of Israel's story points to one thing: Christ. And, more specifically, peace through Christ.

As René Girard points out: "When Jesus declares that he does not abolish the Law but fulfills it, he articulates a logical consequence of his teaching. The goal of the Law is peace among humankind."[7]

That is *the key* right there!

The Law's command to take "an eye for an eye and a tooth for a tooth," rather than being viewed as simply an archaic form of justice, should be viewed as a mandate that actually *attempts* to get to the root of the problem—*violence*. That is to say, it takes us from a more violent place to a less violent one. Remember, once Abel's blood is spilled, vengeance is taken by Lamech—who is only a few generations removed from Abel—seventy times sevenfold (Gen 4:23–24). That is quite a bit more excessive than "an eye for an eye," is it not? Because of this, a flood of violence ensues, wiping out almost all of humanity. To stop such chaos, Mosaic Law gets to the heart of the matter by saying "stop at an eye for an eye," but simply cannot quite do the job (in chapter 3, we'll discuss why). Jesus, however, as the *telos* of the Law, does. And he does so by teaching that we should not resist[8] our persecutors (Matt 5:38–42), that we should love our enemies (v.44), and pray for them, and that we should be perfect, just as our heavenly Father is perfect (v.48). In Luke's version of the sermon, the Father's mercy is the lynchpin of perfection (Luke 6:36), thus showing how mercy and love go hand in hand, and that they are to take precedence *over* retributive justice.

So, does Jesus abolish the Law? No, of course not. Abolishment means that something ends prematurely. He fulfills and exegetes it perfectly. And in doing so, he models a perfect theological framework by showing how God is best defined by his perfect love of enemies (Matt 5:43–48) and mercy for the wicked (Luke

6:36). And he shows that although it may not have *always* been the Moses way—although it is at times—it is in fact the truly human and therefore truly divine Way.

INSTANCE 4: LUKE 20:41–47, REFERENCING PSALM 110:1

This scene begins with "the chief priests and the scribes" questioning Jesus (Luke 20:1). These folks had a tendency for doing such a thing. And not only that, but they also had a tendency to proof-text the Torah during their interrogations, often times in order to then clobber people over the head (John 8:3–5). This led to some atrocious sociological implications (women being stoned to death, for example).

Adding fuel to the fire, in the minds of some, Israel's future king—the messianic deliverer who would free the Jews from the grip of Roman Law—was soon coming with *violence* and *vengeance*, and from the house of David (2 Sam 7:1–17). In spite of Jerusalem being destroyed by the Babylonians in 586 BCE, which forced the Israelites into exile for the next five-hundred or so years, many still believed in this deliverance to come. And that meant there would be hell to pay for Israel's enemies. The Pharisees, no doubt, would have been familiar with this notion, and so too Jesus. In fact, Jesus—while not affirming all the presupposed ideas about what messiahship meant—does accept this title in Mark 14:62.

So, with these two things in mind—the Pharisaical approach to the Scriptures as well as the Davidic understanding of Messiah—let's get to the passage at-hand, because what Jesus does with the Pharisees' inquires is nothing short of brilliant.

After Jesus puts the scribes in their place, Luke tells us how "they no longer dared to ask him another question" (Luke 20:40). Jesus then poses his own rhetorical question: "How can they say that the Messiah is David's son?" Well, certainly Jesus knew that the Messiah *would* come from the Davidic line, *so where is Jesus going with this? What is he up to, asking such a rhetorical question?* He continues:

> "For *David himself says* in the book of the Psalms,
> 'The Lord said to my Lord,
> Sit at my right hand,
> Until I make your enemies your footstool.'"
>
> —Luke 20:41–43, emphasis mine

Let's unpack this by focusing on two distinct things.

First, in Psalm 110:1—the passage being quoted by Jesus—the traditional understanding of this passage is that the first "Lord" mentioned is to be understood as God, while the second is either David or one of his descendants (i.e., a future king).[9]

But this is read differently by Jesus.

When Jesus gets a hold of this passage, he names David as the first "Lord"—*for David himself says*—and the future Messiah (Jesus) as the second. Jesus then asks, "How can they say that the Messiah is David's son?" Why does he ask this? Because, for David to call one of his descendants "lord," it is only because *that* descendant was special in some way, that he was deserving of such a title—you simply did not call your sons and other descendants "lord." To that end, when Jesus attaches *himself* to the second "lord," he is making a dangerously bold move, not only because he tinkers with Scripture in order to do so, but because he is not held in too high of esteem amongst the scribes and Pharisees. If you recall, it is only a few verses prior that they had sent spies to watch Jesus in order to trap him so as to hand him over to the Roman authorities (Luke 20:20). So, for Jesus to attach himself to the concept of "messiah?" Whoa boy, watch out; shit's about to get real!

Second, when Jesus quotes from Psalm 110, he again omits any of the associated vengeance texts (Ps 110:2–3, 5–7). In fact, *any time* Psalm 110 is quoted in the New Testament, Psalm 110:2–3, 5–7 are always omitted (Heb 5:6; 6:20; 7:17, 21). This is important because crucial to any Davidic understanding of messiahship is a Rambo-style deliverance—think along the lines of Mark Driscoll's Jesus: "a Pride fighter with a tattoo down his leg, a sword in his hand and the commitment to make someone bleed."[10] It certainly seems like that is what John the Baptist was expecting (Luke 3:7–9). And it is *definitely* what the folks in Nazareth were waiting for (Luke 4:18–30). But, by attaching himself to the concept of Messiah, and then by again omitting all of the associated vengeance passages from his quotations of Scripture, Jesus reorients the assumed understanding of "divine deliverance." Yes, the Messiah may in fact be from the Davidic line (although perhaps not in the traditional sense), but he will not be a Davidic warrior-type, and he will not be bringing vengeance upon his enemies. Instead, he will love his enemies

> By attaching himself to the concept of Messiah, and then by again omitting all of the associated vengeance passages from his quotations of Scripture, Jesus reorients the assumed understanding of "divine deliverance."

and pray for those who persecute him (Matt 5:44). In fact, Jesus' last prayer prior to his final breath is for the forgiveness of those who declared him an enemy: "Father forgive them; for they do not know what they are doing (Luke 23:34)." What a complete reversal of what Messiah was to be viewed as, a Christology that is a complete rejection of militarism and violent deliverance!

Paul

INSTANCE 5: GALATIANS 3:10-13, REFERENCING DEUTERONOMY 21:23

Paul's letter to the Galatians is one of my favorites. Perhaps it is because we can easily tell just how pissed off Paul is. And, if I'm being honest, that is one of the reasons I like him so much. Like me, he defends the Gospel by telling it like it is and has a bit of a snarky streak. I mean, it is not that often you hear good men of God sarcastically wishing for teachers of false gospels to castrate themselves (Gal 5:12). The last I checked, telling church leaders to cut off their genitalia was frowned upon.

Nevertheless, allow me to offer a brief contextual note so that we can address the passage at-hand.

What is specifically going on in this letter is that Paul is upset by a group of teachers from the Jerusalem Church who are espousing a counterfeit, Jewish-Christian message to his churches in Galatia and elsewhere (Gal 1:7; cf. Rom 16:17). Peter, at least indirectly, is included among these.[11] What is being falsely taught is that prior to becoming a follower of Christ, one had to comply with Mosaic Law: obey the Sabbath, keep a kosher table (Gal 2:11-12), and, if male, become circumcised (Acts 11:2-3;

15:1–2). Furthermore, it seems this false message included some harsh and unfair rhetoric levied against Gentiles.[12] This leads to division in the Church, and really pisses Paul off because for him, there were to be absolutely no dividing lines (Gal 3:28; Rom 10:12), and anything "of the Law" is not to be held in too high esteem—as it brings a curse (Gal 3:10), on Christ even (Gal 3:13), wrath (Rom 4:15), and death (Rom 7:9–10; 8:2). Hence the reason for Paul's rhetoric against the false teachers and their law-based "gospel" in Galatians 5:12: "I wish those who unsettle you would castrate themselves!" In essence, I believe Paul is saying: *If you are going to force people to cut off the tips of their penises in order to be "justified" before God and the Law, then why don't you just go ahead and cut off your own dick instead!*

With this brief contextual note in mind, let's turn to a passage in Galatians where Paul employs a creative interpretation of a familiar phrase from the book of Deuteronomy. He does this in order to condemn the very Law that the false teachers are using in their condemnation of others—which, incidentally, by its very logic, condemns the false teachers themselves (cf. Rom 2:1).

> If you are going to force people to cut off the tips of their penises in order to be "justified" before God and the Law, then why don't you just go ahead and cut off your own dick instead!

Notice how, in Galatians 3:10, Paul emphatically states that the law—which, by the way, Pauline scholar J. Louis Martyn argues was given at Sinai in God's *absence* (Gal 3:19–20)[13]—is a curse to everyone who relies on it (Gal 3:10). Why? Because the

Scriptures are clear: *everyone* will fall short in one way or another (Rom 3:23) and the minute that happens is the minute you are under its curse (Gal 3:10; cf. Deut 28:15, 20–24, 59–61).

After establishing this sobering truth, Paul then lays down the gauntlet by creatively quoting Deuteronomy 21:23, writing: "Cursed is everyone who hangs on a tree" (Gal 3:13). What Paul *fails* to include in that phrase is the kicker. Notice the difference:

- Deuteronomy 21:23: "For anyone hung on a tree is under *God's curse*" (emphasis mine).

- Galatians 3:13: "Cursed is everyone who hangs on a tree."

Did you catch that? For the writer of the book of Deuteronomy—as well as all the penal substitution folks—God's curse is upon anyone who is hung on a tree. But, for Paul, that is not so. In fact, he says that nobody speaking by the Spirit of God says "Jesus is cursed," only that he is Lord (1 Cor 12:3). Yet cursed and hung upon a tree is exactly where Jesus ends up anyway—with help from the Law, no less. So, what Paul understands is that it is not God who is the architect of such cursing—as God does not create systems that lead to the killing of his very own son—but rather, the Law is. Or, to put it really simply, humanity and its systems cursed Jesus. Yet, because he was truly innocent, God raised him from the dead (Gal 1:1); which he would have never done had he really been cursed by God.

INSTANCE 6: ROMANS 15:7–13, REFERENCING VARIOUS PASSAGES FROM PSALM 18; DEUTERONOMY 32:43

We again turn to the Apostle Paul, but this time to his letter to the Romans. It is a most difficult letter to interpret and has given scholars and lay Christians alike fits for millennia. Perhaps it is one of the letters Peter is referring to in 2 Peter 3:16, when he writes, "There are some things in them [Paul's letters] hard to understand." So, for our purposes, we are going to have to make an assumption, namely that Pauline scholar Douglas Campbell is essentially correct in how to best approach it. As a non-scholar myself, I realize that, inevitably, trust will have to be placed in another who is above my pay grade. Do we all not have to do this in some regard? I am not making a blind assumption though. Rather, it is the result of years of diligent study. Perhaps I am wrong, but you will have to decide that for yourself.

So, here's the gist of how Romans is to be approached, according to Campbell and others.[14]

In *The Deliverance of God*, Campbell argues that, instead of all of Romans 1–4 being entirely the "voice of Paul," it is a "dialogue" between Paul and the false teachers we just discussed—those who were either in Rome or on their way to Rome at the time of this letter. Campbell sums up his method for approaching the first four chapters of the letter:

> There are certain instances where Paul attributes material to the Teacher directly, using the technique of prosopopoeia. In these texts the Teacher in effect speaks for himself (although suitably crafted by Paul, of course)—first in the opening of his usual conversion speech (1:18–32), and then later in dialogue with Paul (3:1–9). However, for much of the rest of the argument Paul is quoting the Teacher's teaching, and rather sarcastically, and this is entirely consistent with his main rhetorical goal throughout the section, which is to refute the Teacher in terms of his own gospel.[15]

Remember, this so-called "gospel" is the Jewish-centered one, which, in all reality, is entirely counterfeit (Gal 1:6–7). In addition to keeping various Jewish laws, this *false* gospel comes chock full of anti-Gentile rhetoric, typical of some prominent Jewish sentiments (cf. Wisdom of Solomon 13–14). This rhetoric can be found scattered all throughout Romans 1:18–32. And crucial to this message is the commonly held Jewish belief that "the wrath of God" will be revealed against those Gentiles who practice these abominable things (Rom 1:18).

But, here's where things get good.

Paul, in order to show how false this "gospel" truly is, then turns it right back around on the false teachers in Rom 2:1: "*Therefore* you have no excuse, whoever you are, when you judge others; for in passing judgment on another you condemn yourself, because you, *the judge*, are doing the very same things." (Emphasis mine) Basically, what he is arguing is that if the wrath of God is going to be revealed—just as the false gospel says it is (Rom 1:18)—it will be revealed against the false teachers, too. There is a qualification, however, because in all reality, it will not be the "wrath of God" that befalls the teachers, but wrath stored up by themselves for their insistence on preaching and practicing the gospel of wrath (Rom 2:5). In effect, Paul is saying that you reap what you sow, and if you are going to sow a law-based, wrathful gospel, that is what you are going to reap upon *yourself.*

That being said, let's move on to my main point, which is that Paul then later uses a specific hermeneutical method—similar to that of Jesus in Luke 7:22—as further evidence that the true Gospel is wholly inclusive to Gentiles, and that the false, wrathful, law-based message of the teachers is *dead on arrival*. What he specifically does is quote the Hebrew Scriptures, and then exegetes them so he can point to a time where Gentiles "might glorify God for his *mercy*" (Rom 15:9, emphasis mine). First up, Romans 15:9b (quoting Psalm 18:49): "Therefore I will confess you among the Gentiles, and sing praises to your name." What is left off, of course, is all of the vengeful passages that precede this declaration: "~~They cried for help, but there was no one to save them; they cried to the Lord, but he did not answer them. I beat them fine, like dust before the wind; I cast them out like the mire of the streets…Blessed be… the God who gave me vengeance and subdued peoples under me~~" (Ps 18:41–42, 46–47). Then, one verse later (quoting Deuteronomy 32:43): "And again he says, 'Rejoice, O Gentiles, with his people." And again, what is left off is the vengeance that follows: "~~For he will avenge the blood of his children, and take vengeance on his adversaries; he will repay those who hate him, and cleanse the land for his people.~~"

This consistent interpretive pattern is, again, for the purpose of eliminating the dividing lines that certain Jewish-Christians were creating in the first century. Being falsely taught was that one must obey the Law—kosher table, Sabbath, and penis slicing—in order to have the Gospel. And Paul was having none of it, because, for Paul, to take away the truth of the Gospel with laws fabricated in God's absence (Gal 3:19–20[16]) was to preach a false gospel and thus pronounce judgment on all, including one's self (Rom 2:1). Or, in other words, *to store up self-inflicted wrath* (Rom 2:5).

Yet, for Paul, in spite of all this, due to the fact that all of us, both Jew and Gentile, are so damn disobedient (Rom 11:30–31), God will be merciful to all whom he pleases, that is, *all* (Rom 11:32). *This even includes the false teachers!* That's just how inclusive Paul's theology is. Indeed, it's a theology centered on the mercy of God: "For God has imprisoned all in disobedience so that he may be merciful to all." (Rom 11:32) Hence the jubilant exaltation at the very end of his rhetorical argument (which runs from Romans 9–11): "O the depth of the riches and wisdom and knowledge of God! How unsearchable are his judgments and how inscrutable his ways! 'For who has known the mind of the Lord? Or who has been his counselor? Or who has given a gift to him, to receive a gift in return?' For from him and through him and to him are all things. To him be the glory forever. Amen" (Rom 11:33–36).

INSTANCE 7: EPHESIANS 6:13-17, REFERENCING ISAIAH 59:17-18

Ephesians 6:13–17 is a passage from Paul that should be familiar to any Christian. It reads:

> Therefore take up the whole armor of God, so that you may be able to withstand on that evil day, and having done everything, to stand firm. Stand therefore, and fasten the belt of truth around your waist, and put on the breastplate of righteousness. As shoes for your feet put on whatever will make you ready to proclaim the gospel of peace. With all of these, take the shield of faith, with which you will be able to quench all the flaming arrows of the evil one. Take the helmet of salvation, and the sword of the Spirit, which is the word of God.

What many of us may not realize is that this is a direct reference to Isaiah 59:17–18. However, like so many other instances, there is going to be some tinkering done by Paul. Sure, the "breastplate of righteousness" and "helmet of salvation" are included in Paul's version of the armor of God, but notice what is, not coincidentally, missing:

> "~~He put on garments of vengeance for clothing,~~
>   ~~and wrapped himself in fury as a mantle.~~
> ~~according to their deeds, so he will repay,~~
>   ~~wrath to his adversaries, requital to his enemies.~~"
> —Isaiah 59:17b–18

Indeed, as Paul notes, there is armor to be put on, for there is a war at-hand. However, this is not a war of "blood and flesh," but a war fought against the "cosmic powers of this present darkness, against the spiritual forces of evil in the heavenly places (Eph 6:12)." It is not a war to be fought with literal swords, bows and arrows, but a "sword of the Spirit, which is the word of God." And for this war we bear no garments of vengeance, no boots of war; rather, we gird our bare feet with the "gospel of peace."

> For this war we bear no garments of vengeance, no boots of war; rather, we gird our bare feet with the "gospel of peace."

Concluding Thoughts

In this chapter, my goal was to point to some of the direct evidence that both Jesus and the apostle Paul had a method for interpreting the Hebrew Bible. In essence, what we saw was how both draw out the best of their Scriptures in order to point to a heavenly Father who is non-*sacrificial*, non-*vengeful*, and non-*violent*.

To that end what I want to emphasize is this: To take the Bible seriously is to not take everything literally. Sure, some things we should take literally. Jesus told us to literally love our enemies (Matt 5:44; Luke 6:35); he told us to literally bless those who curse us (Luke 6:28); he told us to literally turn the other cheek (Matt 5:39); and he told us to literally be merciful *just like* our heavenly Father is (Matt 5:48; Luke 6:36). But, as for some of the other shit that we've said about God over the millennia—even if we've said it in the Bible—well, now that's a different story. Some of *that* stuff has to be modified in light of Jesus, the most unexpected of messiahs.

3
The Bible: Rated R for Graphic Divine Violence, Disturbing Images, and Strong Language

"While some people argue for a non-violent Jesus, no one would make such a claim about the God of the Hebrew Bible. In traditional Christianity, Jesus is the Incarnate second person of the Trinity. He is divine, co-equal with the Father. As such, Jesus in the New Testament cannot hold a respectful disagreement with Yahweh of the Old Testament."[1]

—JEFFREY MANN

"Do not resist an evildoer. But if anyone strikes you on the right cheek, turn the other also…love your enemies and pray for those who persecute you, so that you may be children of your Father in heaven."

—JESUS, IN MATTHEW 5:38; 44-45

"The Lord said to Moses, 'Take all the chiefs of the people, and impale them in the sun before the Lord, in order that the fierce anger of the Lord may turn away from Israel…Taking a spear in his hand, [Phinehas] went after the Israelite man into the tent, *and pierced the two of them, the Israelite and the woman, through the belly... The Lord spoke to Moses, saying... "I hereby grant him my covenant of peace."*

—NUMBERS 25:4, 7–8, 10, 12

Now that we've explored some of Jesus and Paul's hermeneutical patterns, let's dig a little deeper into the Scriptures. We'll do this, not only because the Bible is indeed important, but also because for most Protestants, everything seems to begin and end with the "good book." One could call this having a very high view of Scripture—as in Tommy Chong high. It is so high, even, that most of our churches' doctrinal statements, at least here in the United States, begin not with Jesus, but with the Bible—or what they would call "the word." And yes, contained in the Bible is a litany of claims about God that make him out to be, well, if I'm being honest, a raging, murderous sociopath. And before you crucify me for saying that, let's take a look at a few examples of this.

First, turn your attention to Numbers 25. Our story begins with a plague befalling Israel over the fact that God is mad that some of the people have started making sacrifices to other gods. You know, because he's jealous and zealous and all that jazz (Exod 34:14). Due to this, he commands Moses to have these wicked traitors "impaled in the sun" in hopes that his anger would be assuaged (Num 25:4). After a Midianite woman is "brought in" by an Israelite man, Aaron's grandson Phinehas does just as God instructs—he rams his spear through their bellies. *Huzzah!* This pleases God, and so the plague of vengeance that killed 24,000 Israelites is lifted (Num 25:8–9). Due to Phinehas' great zeal for the Lord, he is given a "covenant of peace" and a "covenant of perpetual priesthood." Now, let me reiterate that in case it did not sink in the first time: Phinehas is given a *covenant of peace*, by God, for *killing an interracial couple* who are said to be partially, if not fully, responsible for a *divinely-mandated plague* that, when it was all said and done, killed *24,000 people*.

But wait, there's more.

Head over to Deuteronomy 20. Here we have some rules for how Israel was to properly conduct warfare while taking back the "promised land." What is made clear is that God has a plan for the Canaanites as well as a few of the other "-ites"—including the cute, chubby-cheeked little children. Oh, and all the animals, too! He wants them all *dead*—every man, woman, and yes, *child*. And donkey. And goat. And cow. And…well, you get the picture. I can imagine an angry, white-haired Zeus-like figure, foaming at the mouth:

> "Moses, get your ass over here! Listen up. 'As for the towns of these people that I am giving you as an inheritance, you must not let *anything* that breathes remain alive. You shall annihilate them—the Hittites and the Amorites, the Canaanites and the Perizzites, the Hivites and the Jebusites—just as I have commanded, so that they may not teach you to do all the abhorrent things that they do for their gods [*You mean like kill babies?*], and you thus sin against the Lord your God'" (Deut 20:16–18, emphasis mine).

We have a word for this: *genocide*. Explain it away however you like, but that's what it is. And this is not the only place where God is portrayed as a bloodthirsty, genocidal maniac. In fact, that portrayal is littered all throughout the Hebrew Scriptures, especially in Joshua, Judges, and 1 and 2 Samuel.

Yet, in spite of all this brutality and bloodlust, the story that really gets to me—and in fact is the one that, at one point, broke the camel's back for my faith—is the little-known tale about

Onan. It comes from Genesis 38. Here is a brief synopsis: God kills a wicked man named Er (we're off to a smashing start, are we not?). This makes Er's wife a childless widow. As was the custom, Onan, the brother of the slain Er, was to bear a child with Er's wife. However, Onan is not having any of it so he "pulls out" early, ejaculating on the ground. God then gets pissed and kills Onan too, leaving Judah with two dead sons (as well as a bunch of semen and blood to mop up).

The end.

These are just a few of the many examples to choose from. I could have gone on and on. So, what gives? How can God be said to be so violent, while at the same time that the nonviolent Jesus of Nazareth was, as Paul so clearly put it, the *fullness* of God in bodily form (Col 2:9)? How can God be said to have struck down Uzzah for trying to save the Ark of the Covenant from crashing to the ground (2 Sam 6:7), for example, when Jesus defines God's perfection by his love of enemies (Matt 5:43–48) as well as his mercy (Luke 6:36)? His mercy, people! It seems Uzzah—*who was really only trying to help*—could have been afforded some of that merciful love Jesus spoke about, even if he did happen to break God's command with regard to the proper handling of the Ark.

> The Bible is not inerrant. It is not a part of the Holy Trinity—if it were, we would have to call it the Quadrinity.

So again, what gives?

Well, here is what I see as the crux of the matter. The Bible is not inerrant. It is not a part of the Holy Trinity—if it were, we would have to call it the Quadrinity. But it isn't any such thing.

It is not perfect, and doesn't claim to be! There are "contradictions," if one wants to call them that. Nevertheless, there *are* theological claims that are simply untrue. However—and this is a huge however—there *is* a theological progression—one that actually takes us away from divine violence—found in the Bible. Let's take a look at one example of what I mean by this.

In 2 Kings 9, there is an account of a great massacre at Jezreel by the hands of a man named Jehu. What happens is that Jehu is ordered—nay, *anointed*—by the prophet Elijah to strike down the entire house of his master Ahab over their tyranny and wickedness (2 Kgs 9:7–8). So, he does! And he is championed as a righteous man of God for doing so.[2]

A few generations later, however, the prophet Hosea sees things differently. Speaking on behalf of the Lord, Hosea writes: "For in a while I will punish the house of Jehu for the blood of Jezreel, and I will put an end to the kingdom of the house of Israel" (Hos 1:4). In other words, according to Hosea, God is not all-too-pleased with what the murderous zealot Jehu did to the house of Ahab. This, in spite of Elijah's commanding such a thing.

This move away from violence is a key component to the overarching biblical metanarrative, but it is a move that is far from a neatly drawn straight line. Rather, the Bible is a "text in travail,"[3] as René Girard calls it, and as such what needs to happen is that the Bible needs to be "rightly divided" (2 Tim 2:15). As we explored in the last chapter, that does not mean we can simply split up the "testaments" while keeping to the mantra "God said it, I believe it, and that settles it." Rather, we need to rightly divide between what can be called religion and revelation, sacred violence and divine shalom, the voice of the retributive victim and the voice of the forgiving one.

So, where is a good place to begin when thinking about this?

Well, becoming privy to how human beings behave, structure our societies, develop our religions, and how we tell our stories, is a fantastic jumping off point. For if we do not understand our anthropological realities, that is, if we do not understand what it means to be human, how can we not *misunderstand* any theological realities, or simply, what it means for God to be God?

With that being said, we will begin with a crash course in René Girard's mimetic theory, staring with a discussion about human desire.

As Aristotle points out in Book IV of *Poetics*, the human being is an imitative creature, and strongly so. I am oversimplifying things, but after our basic needs like food, water, and shelter are met, we typically don't know what to desire. So, what we do is non-consciously model for one another which objects should be deemed the most desirable as well as which ones should not. Girard explains it like this:

> We are constituted by the other, that is, by parents, authority figures, peers, rivals whom we internalize as models and who become the unconscious basis of our desires. This does not mean that freedom of the will is not possible. Humankind as created in the image of God is not intended to be *identical* to the other or exist in *slavish subservience* to the other. However, since we learn first and primarily through mimesis, our freedom depends on being constituted by the other.[4]

What Girard is saying is that any freedom this "self" has is because we share desires with the other, otherwise our desires would be on fixed objects, or in other words, a form of instinct.[5]

Pay attention to the fashion industry, which uses celebrities and other various stars to model their clothing. They do so in the hope that we will all desire their brand simply because those we look up to—guys like Tom Brady, for example—desire that brand (or so we convince ourselves after we watch their commercials). And this works! Why? Because our desires are such that they become non-consciously fueled and flamed by "the other"—those we can't help but take on as models. For another example, ask yourself what tends to happen when two children are in a room full of toys. More often than not, will they not end up fighting over a single toy? It does not really matter which toy, either, as conflict comes to fruition as soon as one child shows interest in a particular toy, and the other child, via mimetic desire, wants that same toy. Oh, but let's not just blame children for this. Adults are just as culpable. Have you read the national newspapers around "Black Friday?" Or, heaven forbid, been involved in the mayhem? The shiny toys we grown-ups so desperately need—items like big screen TVs, tablets, and gaming systems—cause us to trample each other to death in order to get one of the few blockbuster deals.

The Decalogue's tenth command gets to the very heart of this matter. When the writer says "thou shalt not *covet*"—or in other words, *desire*, as the Hebrew word *chamad* can mean either—they are speaking to a fundamental human problem, namely the problem of desire. Notice how the commandment is laid out in Exodus 20:17. After going through all the objects we are to avoid desiring, the writer seems to give up, conceding that what needs to be prohibited is whatever belongs to the neighbor.[6] It doesn't matter what the object is; it is the neighbor's ownership that gives the objects their powerfully desirable effect.

Yet, to this day, we continue to engage in the very mimetic conflicts the Decalogue is warning us about. We do this, not only because it is simply who we are, but because prohibitions do not really work at quelling violence entirely. In fact, they are like the Greek *pharmakon*—both the *poison* and the *antidote*. Think about what happens when people are told not to push the "red button," or when children are told not to touch the hot stove, or when Adam and Eve are prohibited from eating the fruit of a certain tree (Gen 2—3). I could go on, but I think the answers are fairly obvious.

> When societal violence escalates to the point of spiraling out of control, people turn to a surrogate victim to place their hostility on. In doing this, they unify against this enemy "other."

We just can't help ourselves! We have to push the button, touch the stove, and eat the fruit.

Due to the fact that making something taboo is not the end-all-be-all solution to repressing mimetic violence, we continue in our violent ways—so much so that throughout history entire societies and civilizations have wiped themselves out through violent in-fighting, cannibalized out of existence.

But, not all of them. Why?

Here's an analogy: human societies are like pressure-cookers. Some have faulty release valves, so will eventually and violently explode. But others have a perfectly functioning pressure release valve. What is this mechanism for relieving the pressure of societal violence? In a word: *scapegoating*.

When societal violence escalates to the point of spiraling out of control, people turn to a surrogate victim to place their hostility on. In doing this, they unify against this enemy "other." We witnessed this in 2011 after Osama bin Laden was killed. A nation divided along party lines—Democrat Blue and Republican Red—powerfully came together in the city streets to sing the national anthem and "God Bless America." We did this because Bin Laden was like a virus, a plague, the face of evil; he was the entire Western world's *persona non grata*, public enemy number one. This, we could all agree on! So, through the scapegoating of Bin Laden,[7] a nation divided became, at least for a brief moment in time, a nation united.

When we think about archaic societies, then, it is easy to imagine how this process of unification was believed to be divinely mandated (as if that doesn't happen today). We see this truth in our many ancient stories and legends. In the Oedipus myth, for example, the Apollonian plague is not lifted until *after* a "guilty" King Oedipus is expelled from Thebes. Similarly, in Numbers 25, the plague the Israelites were under is lifted after Phinehas murders a "guilty" interracial couple (Num 25:8).

As Girard noticed, this is the theme of many of humanity's myths, because, as the saying goes, "dead men tell no tales." In myth after myth, we have papered over the truth of our victimizing by claiming our violence is sacred, and that we needed it in order to be spared from something dreadful, while those whom we have victimized remain forever silenced, six feet under, or at minimum, far removed from society. Then, almost ironically, because our victims are attached to the ensuing peace, we sometimes even deify them.

This is seen, quite pointedly, in the myth of Maria Lionza.[8] In one account of this tale, it is said that the daughter of the Caquetio Indian chief—because of her being born with green eyes (a sign that she was perhaps a spy for the invading

Spanish[9])—is delivered over to an anaconda that lived at the bottom of a lake. After she is thrown in, however, she comes right back up to the surface, not in the same manner that she went in, but as an exquisite goddess encircled by multitudes of animals, waters, and plants. So, in other words, she is scapegoated and killed because she is just a bit different than the rest of the society—green eyes rather than a darker color like most Caquetio Indians—and in her sacrificial slaying, rises to god-status. Hence, like many other mythical gods, Maria Lionza is the *pharmakon*, the poison and the antidote.

In order for a society to keep the peace as long as humanly possible, we tend toward ritualizing this process of societal bloodletting, which gives birth to the altar of sacrifice—the lynchpin of religion, archaic and otherwise. In our minds: *If the killing of a surrogate victim (scapegoat) brought peace the first time, other events like that should work thereafter.* That is why blood sacrifices often reenact, insofar as they are able, the original killing. I'll quote Girard at-length to explain how this happens:

> To understand how these rituals are born, let us imagine a community's state of mind when, after a period of bloody conflict, it is delivered from its misfortune by an unexpected mob action. In the early days or months that followed this deliverance, it is likely that a great euphoria prevailed. But sadly this blessed period never lasted. Humans are so constituted that they always fall back into their mimetic rivalries. "Scandal must come," and it always does occur, sporadically at first, and little attention is paid to it. But soon it begins to proliferate. Now those affected must face facts: a new crisis threatens the community. How to prevent this disaster? The community has not forgotten the strange, incomprehensible drama that sometime ago drew it up from the abyss, where the community now fears it will fall again.

It is full of gratitude toward the mysterious victim who plunged it initially into that disaster but who subsequently saved it.

When the people involved reflect on these strange events, they must say to one another that if the whole process unfolded as it did, it was without doubt because the mysterious victim wanted it that way. Perhaps this god has organized this entire scenario with the purpose of arousing his new worshippers to reproduce it and renew its effects so that in the future they will be protected from a possible recurrence of mimetic disorder.[10]

Although many of the world's religions have unique characters and rituals, the deep-seeded truth behind them is the same, which is, the practice of sacrifice assumes an original murder. That is to say human religion and culture are founded on violence. The many founding myths—Cain and Abel (Hebrew), Romulus and Remus (Roman), Cadmus and the Dragon (Greek), and so on—all speak to this.

But here is where the Bible parts ways with other ancient writings: it includes the voice of the victim. And more than that! The Bible includes the voice of the *forgiving* victim. Sure, the Bible ebbs and flows, and includes many stories where the victor and persecutor is championed—as in the Israelites' victory over the Canaanites, Phinehas' slaying of the Israelite/Midianite couple, and David's sacrificing a host of Israelites to the Gibeonites (2 Sam 21:1–9)—but it focuses quite heavily on including the voice of the persecuted as well. To understand what I mean by this, let's begin by looking at the story of Cain and Abel.

This tale is not unlike other founding murder myths. For example, legend has it that Rome is founded only after two brothers, Romulus and Remus, bicker over how to interpret an omen. Romulus slays his brother, and then goes on to be the hero of the story, founding what would become arguably the world's greatest empire. The Hebrew Scriptures put a twist in the tale though. In the biblical story, the voice of the slaughtered victim can be heard (Gen 4:10). The slain Abel cries out for vengeance! But God is not having any of it, and in spite of Cain being entirely guilty of the murder, puts a mark on him in hopes that violence will stop dead in its tracks (Gen 4:15). As we all probably know, this doesn't work. In a handful of generations, a man named Lamech is taking vengeance on others at a rate of seventy-sevenfold, and by the time we meet Noah, violence and corruption are so prevalent that it overwhelms humanity in a flood of epic proportions.

Fast forward a few thousand years to Jesus. Like Abel, the first century itinerant preacher from Nazareth is murdered in cold blood. Both the dying bandit on the cross and the Roman centurion testify to this (Luke 23:41, 47). Yet, *unlike* Abel, the blood of the slain Jesus does not cry for vengeance from the grave. In fact, as the writer of Hebrews puts it, the blood of Jesus "speaks a better word than the blood of Abel" (Heb 12:24). How do we know? The Resurrection. Only three days after his death, Jesus is raised in order to speak the good word of shalom, of forgiveness. Whereas the voice of religion always speaks the language of death and sacrifice, and whereas most human victims cry for retribution and vengeance, the voice of divine revelation transcends this by speaking the language of life, by the pouring out of one's self in love for the other. John 20:19–23 captures this beautifully:

> When it was evening on that day, the first day of the week, and the doors of the house where the disciples had met were locked for fear of the Jews, Jesus came and stood among them and said, "Peace be with you." After he said this, he showed them his hands and his side. Then the disciples rejoiced when the saw the Lord. Jesus said to them again, "Peace be with you. As the Father has sent me, so I send you." When he had said this, he breathed on them and said to them, "Receive the Holy Spirit. If you forgive the sins of any, they are forgiven them; if you retain the sins of any, they are retained."

It is here where we are introduced to what Catholic theologian James Alison calls "the intelligence of the victim."[11] Because of the Resurrection, for the first time in human history we can see just how wrong we've been doing things—our Victim is vindicated. We can see, with clarity, how human kingdoms, being structured on the sacrificial principle, are contradictory to the kingdom of God, which is instead structured on the self-emptying love and grace of the Father, Son, and Spirit. That is Gospel, dear friends. That is good news, which is no better explained than by Michael Hardin in the following:

> Jesus' blood covers our sin, not through some divine forensic transaction but as we lift our blood-stained hands we hear the divine voice 'You are forgiven, each and every one of you, all of you.'…The cross of Christ is the place of revelation, the resurrection of Jesus is the vindication of that revelation, and the ascension, where Jesus is given the Unpronounceable Name (Phil 2:5–11) is the place where that revelation is confirmed for all time. This is the good news, this is the gospel.[12]

Because of Jesus, we have a chance to enter into a new type of human community. The breaking of bodies can be replaced by the breaking of bread. The pouring out of our victims' blood can be replaced by the pouring out of a fine cabernet sauvignon. May we have eyes to see and ears to hear what story the Bible, rightly divided, is really telling.

4
Marcionite! An In-vogue Strawman

"*French scholar René Girard says, 'In the OT we never arrive at a conception of the deity that is entirely foreign to violence...Only the text of the Gospels manage to achieve what the OT leaves incomplete.' Obviously, this pseudo-scholar hasn't done his homework; maybe he is just lazy. If someone would point him to my blog he can skip reading the Bible, since obviously he has never done so a day in his life.*"[1]

—BILLY DYER

"*Girard's wholly loving, nonviolent God is uncomfortably similar to Marcion's God.*"[2]

—CALEB NELSON

I've been called a Marcionite more times than I can remember. And not just me, but pretty much all of my mentors, colleagues, and friends, too! In fact, this accusation seems to be leveled against *anyone* who says that "God is just like Jesus" and/or questions any or all of the divine violence espoused in the Scriptures. However, if I may be frank, this indictment is, at best, nothing more than a strawman logical fallacy, in which the *God-is-just-like-Jesus-position* is misrepresented in order to make it easier to attack and refute. And so, like any strawmen, it should be rejected like eight-time NBA All-Star Dikembe Mutombo rejected weak-ass lay-ups in the paint.

To understand just why the charge of Marcionism is fallacious, let's begin by taking a brief look at what, exactly, Marcion of Sinope (80–150 CE) believed. Then, we will compare that with what I, as a Nicene-Creed-believing, fairly orthodox Christian accept as true, in hopes that we can see just how grossly misguided the Marcionism accusation is.

Marcion: Arch-Heretic of the Church

Though there are a number of reasons as to why Marcion was an important figure during the second century, he is now primarily remembered for only one. Yes, he was an gifted thinker and yes, he asked one of the more crucial theological questions one could ask—*how is the violent God of the Jewish Scriptures related to the gracious Father of Jesus?*—but is only really known for the answer he provided: *they are not*. In essence, Marcion's arch-heretic status was achieved because he concluded that the Jewish, creator god was a separate God from the Heavenly Father of Jesus and Paul. German Lutheran theologian Adolf von Harnack explains how Marcion arrived at such a conclusion:

> In the God of the [Old Testament] he [Marcion] saw a being whose character was stern justice, and therefore anger, contentiousness and unmercifulness. The law which rules nature and man appeared to him to accord with the characteristics of this God and the kind of law revealed by him, and therefore it

seemed credible to him that this God is the creator and lord of the world (κοσμοκράτωρ). As the law which governs the world is inflexible and yet, on the other hand, full of contradictions, just and again brutal, and as the law of the Old Testament exhibits the same features, so the God of creation was to Marcion a being who united in himself the whole gradations of attributes from justice to malevolence, from obstinacy to inconsistency.[3]

Without a doubt, the polytheistic nature of this worldview[4]—as well as the intertwined Gnosticism (the created order/flesh=bad, the Spirit world=good)—is more than enough to charge Marcion with heresy. His dismissal of the entirety of the Jewish Scriptures is the icing on the cake.

As an unabashed Girardian, I completely reject this view (not to mention, Marcion's view that not all will be saved!) Never have I espoused anything polytheistic. Never have I said the created order is bad, or even that it is ultimately split from the spiritual order (God is the God of *all*, is he not?) Never have I rejected the God of the Hebrew Scriptures, only some of the theology championed by some of the Jewish writers (but so did the Jewish prophets!) Never have I concluded that the Hebrew Scriptures are entirely wrong, only sometimes so (but so too are some of the New Testament writers).

For one such example, the writer of Deuteronomy 28 paints the following violent picture of God:

1. Deuteronomy 28:15: "If you will not obey the Lord your God by diligently observing all his commandments and decrees, which I am commanding you today, then all these curses shall come upon you and overtake you."

2. Deuteronomy 28:20–24: "The Lord will send upon you disaster, panic, and frustration in everything you attempt to do, until you are destroyed and perish quickly, on account of the evil of your deeds, because you have forsaken me. The Lord will make the pestilence cling to you until it has consumed you off the land that you are entering to possess. The Lord will afflict you with consumption, fever, inflammation, with fiery heat and drought, and with blight and mildew; they shall pursue you until you perish. The sky over your head shall be bronze, and the earth under you iron. The Lord will *change the rain of your land into powder, and only dust shall come down upon you from the sky until you are destroyed* (emphasis mine).

3. Deuteronomy 28:59–61: "The Lord will overwhelm both you and your offspring with severe and lasting afflictions and grievous and lasting maladies. He will bring back upon you all the disease of Egypt, of which you were in dread, and they shall cling to you. Every other malady and affliction, even though not recorded in the book of this law, the Lord will inflict on you until you are destroyed."

I am not sure how else to put it except that this view of God is wrong. Putting Marcion aside for a second, Jesus *himself* shows us *how* by reorienting the theology behind these passages. For example, in John 9:2, Jesus' disciples assume a blind man that they've come across is a sinner (or that his parents are), because they carry with them the cultural and religious assumption that no blind man is in God's good graces. It's the same type of worldview that Job and his "friends" had (Job 4:7–8; 8:20;

11:14–15). And the Pharisees—those we often unfairly view as the "bad guys" in the Gospels[5]—concur with this worldview when they also accuse the blind man of being "born entirely in sins" (John 9:34).

For Jesus, though, this theological assumption is inaccurate: "Neither this man nor his parents sinned: he was born blind so that God's works might be revealed in him" (John 9:3). And the work that God is continually doing is that of healing and reconciliation, most pointedly here when Jesus cures the man of his blindness (John 9:7). Remember, due to this man's condition, he was destined to only fill the role of societal outcast. For the Scriptures were clear: failing to diligently observe all the words of the law resulted in not only severe and lasting afflictions on the sinner, but on his offspring as well (Deut 28:58–59). But this divine cursing is not something Jesus believed was present in his Abba! For Jesus, God does not dry up the rain on the wicked (Deut 28:24); he sends rain on both the righteous *and* the wicked (Matt 5:45). That is to say, God is not a cursing and blessing God, but a blessing God *only*. As the writer of 1 John puts it, "God is light and in him there is no darkness at all" (1 John 1:5).

> For Jesus, God does not dry up the rain on the wicked (Deut 28:24); he sends rain on both the righteous *and* the wicked (Matt 5:45).

However—and this is a huge however—we are not chucking out the entire Hebrew Bible, as Marcion did. That is not what Jesus did, it is not what Paul or the writer to the Hebrews did, nor is it what we are doing. I, for one, simply see the dying, rising, and forgiving Christ as the lens through which we view the Hebrew Scriptures (i.e. a Cruciform hermeneutic). I kind of thought that was what being a *Christ*-ian was all about. Period. It's certainly the point being made in the story from Luke 24, where the risen Christ—the Vindicated Victim—interprets for the disciples, beginning with Moses and all the prophets, "the things about himself in all the scriptures" (Luke 24:27). What Jesus makes clear is that everything a Christian does and thinks and believes—including what we believe about the Bible—is through the lens of Christ crucified (1 Cor 2:2). We begin talking about God at the cross and go from there, not the other way around (by trying to fit the cross into our presupposed God-concepts). Indeed, this is what Luther meant by a "theology of the cross."[6]

What is striking, then, is that, unlike Marcion, when we *do* use this Cruciform hermeneutic we actually see Christ *throughout the Hebrew Scriptures*. We see a Christ-figure in the Suffering Servant of Second Isaiah, who is sent to the grave as a wicked man, even though "he had done *no violence*" (Isa 53:9, emphasis mine). We witness the themes of forgiveness and reconciliation—themes that pervade Christ's Gospel (Eph 6:15; Col 1:15–20)—in the story of Joseph and his brothers. In this tale, for instance, Joseph's brothers end up bowing to Joseph precisely *because* he forgives their original treachery. This is significant because it stands in contrast to the idea that reconciliation occurs only when a victim is expelled (cf. Num 25:1–13). Such is the case, if you recall, in the myth of Oedipus, where the city of Thebes is saved from a curse only after the people expel a "guilty" Oedipus from their city. But, the Hebrew Scriptures get it right (at times), stepping in and saying "hold on just a minute"—*mercy* and *forgiveness* are what bring true peace (Gen 50:15–21).

That is why we do not throw the Hebrew Scriptures out. They are inspired (2 Tim 3:16). I know Evangelicals will agree with me there. We just may not agree that every writer of every bit of Scripture had the perfect theological framework to work with. But again, this is hardly Marcionism. Rather, it is taking seriously what Paul calls the "Gospel of peace" (Eph 6:15). It is putting peace and reconciliation, as achieved through the blood of the cross (Col 1:20), front and center. It is not assuming God is violent because there are thousands of years of history to suggest so, but rather, it is allowing the True Human who would rather go the cross than engage in violence begin the fully unveiled theological conversation, so to speak.

So, here's the fact of the matter: The violence found in the Hebrew Scriptures will somehow have to be reconciled with the nonviolent rabbi from Nazareth. There really are no two ways about it. The early Church recognized this. Many a Church Father offered ways of going about it. From Justin Martyr to Clement of Alexandria, Irenaeus and Cyprian, various solutions were put forth.[7] But, the one that really stuck was Augustine's. Michael Hardin teaches:

> The majority solution, while rejecting the two gods theory of Marcion, tended to unify all biblical statements about God in just as much of a dualistic paradigm as Marcion's. By the time

we get to Augustine (400 CE), the most influential figure in Christian history after the Apostle Paul, God's character has two sides, light and dark, loving and wrathful, merciful and punishing. This two-faced view of God (the Janus-Face) has dominated Christian theology ever since.[8]

I suppose the best question to ask ourselves is: *Should this be the best way of addressing the problem Marcion was aptly keen to?* When pressed, this solution doesn't seem to hold much water. Not only does it fail in addressing the dualism of Marcion—creating a two-faced god rather than having two gods with two unique names and "faces" hardly counts—but it also fails to fully address the startling Christian claim that the nonviolent, nonretributive, enemy-forgiving Jesus is the *fullness* of God in bodily form (Col 2:9), and that he and the Father are *homoousios* (of the same substance). How so? Because, for my money, if they are of the same substance, they are of the same nature. And if they are of the same nature, then anything contradictory to the nature of Jesus is contradictory to the nature of God—yes, that means even if it clearly says it in the Bible. Which means that Western Christendom's God of two faces needs to scram. He's had his time in the sun. It's time for the Church to embrace the one-natured God that Jesus—the only one to have seen the Father (John 1:18; 6:46)—showed us.

Selah.

> Anything contradictory to the nature of Jesus is contradictory to the nature of God.

5
God made Adam, Eve, *and* Steve

"Homosexuality is clearly condemned in the Bible. It undermines God's created order where he made Adam and Eve, a man and a woman, to carry out the command to fill and subdue the earth (Gen 1:28). Homosexuality cannot fulfill that mandate."[1]

—MATT SLICK

"Homosexuality is a result of the rejection of God (Rom 1:21–25). Gay marriage is the institutionalization of the rejection of God… The Bible teaches how Christians should respond to gay marriage. Don't condone it; no matter how much we may love our friends and want to see them happy, real love is bringing them to a saving relationship with Jesus, not encouraging a sinful lifestyle."[2]

—GOT QUESTIONS MINISTRIES

For the good part of thirty years, I held to the belief that homosexuality was a sin in the eyes of God. I was handed this view from my parents and the evangelical church at an age I cannot remember, and they had it handed to them from people and places of which I could only speculate. In all likelihood, they would tell you that their view came directly from the Bible, but

I have since learned that really should come to mean *their interpretation of the Bible*.

After all, every single one of us, from the conservative premillennial dispensationalist to the liberal Anabaptist, has a hermeneutic. In other words, everyone has a lens through which they view the Bible, whether they admit it or not. I'll even take that one step further. *Everyone* has a lens through which they view *everything*, and so we can never escape our own subjectivity, even when addressing so-called objective truths.

> Out of the over thirty-thousand total verses in the Bible, you can count on two hands how many cover "homosexuality."

To that end, when it comes to a Christian's attitude toward the GSM (Gender and Sexual Minority) community, we must keep this humbly in mind and not be so cavalier about rejecting these folks, labeling them "sinners" based solely on their sexuality or gender identity. To the contrary, it's my strong contention that we actually have a duty to wholly and openly affirm such a group.

The Pesky Bible

The strongest "Christian" case against affirming the GSM community is the Bible. Duh, right? But let me be clear, even *that* case is thin in terms of how much weight is even given to the issue. In fact, out of the over thirty-thousand total verses in the Bible, you can count on two hands how many cover "homosexuality." These are what are commonly known as the "clobber passages."[3]

This raises the question: Why does this topic cause such a stir within Christianity? One would think that Christians would be far more concerned with practicing compassion, kindness, humility, meekness, and patience (Col 3:12), loving thine enemies (Mark 11:25; Matt 5:44; Luke 6:27), helping the poor (Matt 19:21; Gal 2:10), the orphans and widows (Js 1:27), showing mercy and grace to the world (Matt 9:13; Luke 6:36; John 8:1–11), and living in the Spirit, whose fruit includes love, joy, peace, forbearance, kindness, goodness, faithfulness, gentleness, and self-control (Gal 5:22–23). Is this not the overarching message of the Bible, particularly the New Testament?

Furthermore, one only needs a friendly reminder from the Apostle Paul as to why we should not point the accusatory finger at others: "All have sinned and fall short of the glory of God" (Rom 3:23). So, judge not, lest ye be judged (Matt 7:1). This much we should all agree on.

Now, as with anything, context is crucial. As Jarrod Saul McKenna reminds us, "A text without a context is a con."[4] If we miss this, we'll risk missing everything, including how, as post-postmodern followers of Christ, we should approach the fairly modern issue of "homosexuality." For instance, does it make any sense for any Christian to pluck out Old Testament verses from their original historical and cultural context in order to clobber others, given that we are not under the Law but under Grace? It seems it would be a *con* to the very faith we proclaim!

Nevertheless, if we *are* willing to clobber gay people with Leviticus 20:13,[5] for example, are we also willing to be consistent when it comes to tattoos (Lev 19:28), eating bacon-wrapped shrimp (Lev 11:2–11), or wearing cotton/poly blends

(Lev 19:19)? Do we stone women to death if they are found to have lost their virginity prior to being wed (Deut 22:13–21)? Do we execute children for cursing their parents (Exod 21:15)? Do we execute those who break the Sabbath (Exod 31:14)? Do we execute rape victims who don't cry out loud enough whilst being sexually assaulted (Deut 22:23–24)? For the love of God, and I mean that in the sincerest sense, *I hope not!*

Some may be inclined to make the argument that, while we have the authority to eliminate all the ceremonial and cultural laws from our books, we must not touch the moral ones. In other words, Christians can do away with everything culturally "Jewish," but their moral precepts—marriage rites and the like—need to remain. However, as my friend and blogger, Dr. Benjamin L. Corey, reminds us, things aren't so cut and dried:

> This argument presupposes that the Law is divided into categories—mainly dietary, morality, and ceremony. Unfortunately, the Law is *not* sorted into categories. The Law itself does not identify different categories, neither is it written in a way where the laws are sorted into clean and separate categories. For example, there's not a book of food laws followed by a book of moral laws—it's simply not written this way. Can we sort them into categories? Sure, but only for pedagogical purposes, nothing more.[6]

And this isn't even the most damning argument against those who want to split up the Law into neat and tidy categories in order to push what they call "a proper biblical worldview." Far from it. In fact, in Paul's letter to the Galatians—a letter in which he has little good to say about the Law—he tells the church that if they insist on following one law (in this case, male circumcision) they have to follow them all (Gal 5:3).

So, again I ask: If we are willing to anachronistically impose the Law when it comes to marriage rites, are we also willing to impose all the other 613 laws onto others and ourselves? If so, then we are hardly following Paul, given that Paul himself said he was not under the Law (1 Cor 9:20), as it had been cancelled when it was nailed to the cross (Col 2:14). So why in the hell would *we* want to go back?

> If we are willing to anachronistically impose the Law when it comes to marriage rites, are we also willing to impose all the other 613 laws onto others and ourselves?

SHIFTING OUR FOCUS ONTO THE NEW TESTAMENT

The Cultural Context

First, allow me to note that Jesus never once explicitly discusses "homosexuality" or "homosexual marriage." Neither does Paul—not in the way we, in the twenty-first century, would. How could they? These were not classifications present during the first century. Here's how the *Oxford Classical Dictionary* begins its entry on what homosexuality *was* and *was no*t in classical antiquity:

> No Greek or Latin word corresponds to the modern term *homosexuality*, and ancient Mediterranean societies did not in practice treat homosexuality as a socially operative category of personal or public life. Sexual relations between persons of the same sex certainly did occur (they are widely attested in ancient sources), but they were not systematically distinguished or conceptualized as such, much less were they thought to represent a

single, homogeneous phenomenon in contradistinction to sexual relations between persons of different sexes. That is because the ancients did not classify kinds of sexual desire or behavior according to the sameness or difference of the sexes of the persons who engaged in a sexual act; rather, they evaluated sexual acts according to the degree to which such acts either violated or conformed to norms of conduct deemed appropriate to individual sexual actors by reason of their gender, age, and social status...The application of "homosexuality" (and "heterosexuality") in a substantive and normative sense to sexual expression in classical antiquity is not advised.[7]

Now, I don't use this quote in order to suggest that Paul did not warn others about engaging in "male prostitution and sodomy" (1 Cor 6:9; 1 Tim 1:10) or "shameless acts with men" (Rom 1:27[8]), because he did. And strongly so. But, he also warned against a whole host of other immoral acts as well. Again, though, context is crucial.

As I've already noted, the concept of "homosexuality" was not present in Paul's day, at least not in the modern way we view it. So, when Paul talks about unnatural acts between same-sex partners, it seems reasonable to think that he was speaking to something else entirely, something relevant to the issues he would have been facing as a first-century Christian. Pastor John Shore succinctly explains what that was exactly:

> During the time in which the New Testament was written, the Roman conquerors of the region frequently and openly engaged in homosexual acts between themselves and boys. Such acts were also common between Roman men and their male slaves. These acts of non-consensual sex were considered normal and socially acceptable. They were, however, morally repulsive to Paul, as today they would be to everyone, gay and straight.[9]

What Shore is rightly saying is that sexual relationships in the ancient world—not just between men and men, but between men and women as well—tended to be hierarchical: the penetrated being subservient to the penetrator. To that end, being on the receiving end of such a relationship meant one was under the thumb of oppression, under the power of coercion. Indeed, they were often viewed as nothing more than play things by those who lorded over them.

A Brief Look at the Greek Text

"Do you not know that wrongdoers will not inherit the kingdom of God? Do not be deceived! Fornicators, idolaters, adulterers, male prostitutes [malakoi], sodomites [arsenokoitai], thieves, the greedy, drunkards, revilers, robbers—none of these will inherit the kingdom of God."

—1 CORINTHIANS 9:9–10

"This means understanding that the law is laid down not for the innocent but for the lawless and disobedient, for the godless and sinful, for the unholy and profane, for those who kill their father or mother, for murderers, fornicators, sodomites [arsenokoitai], slave traders, liars, perjurers, and whatever else is contrary to the sound teaching that conforms to the glorious gospel of the blessed God, which he untrusted to me."

—1 TIMOTHY 1:9–11

If we break down the actual Greek words used by Paul in places like 1 Corinthians 6:9–10 and 1 Timothy 1:10,[10] we'll certainly notice the same sort of context—a context that has nothing to do with love and partnership, but more to do with coercion and force.

In 1 Corinthians 6:9, for example, the word the NKJV translates as "homosexuals"—it's rendered "male prostitutes" in the NRSV—comes from the Greek word "malakoi," but hardly means what we mean when we say "homosexual." In fact, in Matthew 11:8 and Luke 7:25, Jesus describes some articles of clothing as "malakoi." Or, in other words, "soft." (News break: he's not calling the clothes "gay.") And yet, it indeed can be used to describe people as well. In such instances, however, the correct translation would be more along the lines of "effeminate": prepubescent boys with clean-shaven faces, for instance.[11] As my friend and blogger Keith Giles notices, both Plato and Josephus used the word to describe those who were not yet fit for battle, while Aristotle linked "malakoi" with those who over-indulge in pleasure.[12] The *New American Bible* offers the following definition:

> [Malakoi] may refer to catamites, i.e., boys or young men who were kept for purposes of prostitution, a practice not uncommon in the Greco-Roman world. In Greek mythology, this was the function of Ganymede, the "cupbearer of the gods," whose Latin name was Catamitus. The term translated "sodomites" refers to adult males who indulged in homosexual practices with such boys. See similar condemnations of such practices in Romans 1:26–27; 1 Timothy 1:10.[13]

Hell, even the staunchly conservative Calvinist John MacArthur (aka Johnny Mac) agrees. Describing the first-century Corinthian Christians, he writes:

> They also lived in a society that was notoriously immoral, a society that, in the *temple prostitution* and other ways, actually

glorified promiscuous sex. To have sexual relations with a prostitute was so common in Corinth that the practice came to be called "Corinthianizing." Many believers had formerly been involved in such immorality, and it was hard for them to break with the old ways and easy to fall back in to them… it was also hard for them to give up their sexual immorality (emphasis mine).[14]

So, what does the word really mean?

Well, we cannot be 100 percent certain. But the second word in question—which the NKJV translates as "sodomites"—can help lend a hand. It comes from the Greek word "arsenokoitai."

Now, to be frank, this is not a simple word to translate either. Why? Because it is a word that is hardly used in the Bible. In fact, other than 1 Corinthians 6:9, its only other usage is in 1 Timothy 1:10. And there, its meaning is hardly clear. However, if we focus our attention outside of the Bible for a moment, to Philo—the highly respected Jewish philosopher—things do in fact get a bit clearer.

Commenting on Leviticus 18:22—you know, that "clobber passage" that says it's an abomination for a man to lie down with another man—Philo argues that what is being condemned is "arsenokoitai," which, incidentally, he understands, not as what we would consider "homosexual," but as *shrine prostitution*.[15] That's right, Leviticus 18:22 isn't about being gay, it's about a certain, grotesque version of prostitution. The same thing goes for 1 Corinthians 6:9 and 1 Timothy 1:10; which, not surprisingly, actually fits with the context of both passages—passages, mind you, that have a whole hell of a lot to do with force, coercion, and lording over others.

To that end, the problem for Paul, just as Shore points out above, isn't that it's an abomination for two consenting male adults to engage in a romantic and/or sexual relationship, it's an abomination for men to engage in prostitution (*arsenokoitai*) with effeminate, prepubescent, clean-shaven boys (*malakois*). That is simply to say, it isn't cool to rape little boys and force them to be your sex-slave (I know, shocking, right?).

So, I'm almost forced to ask: *Is this the phenomenon we are witnessing today?* Are non-heterosexual couples clamoring to have the right to coercively engage in sexual acts with unwilling partners? Are they hell-bent on garnering the legal right to participate in pederasty? Of course not! To that end, using the writings of the Apostle Paul outside of the original historical context in order to create *any division* in the body of Christ is not only anachronistic and illogical, but ethically out of line.

As Christians, we should understand this, for it is Paul himself who *plainly* teaches: "There is no longer Jew or Greek, there is no longer slave or free, there is no longer *male* or *female*; for all of you are one in Christ Jesus" (Gal 3:28, emphasis mine). And that isn't to say that Paul is arguing *for* or *against* a proper sexual orientation—again, how could he?—but that there were to be no dividing lines in the Church. Full stop. In the first century, those lines included whether your table was kept Kosher or not, whether you rested on the Sabbath or not, and whether, if male, some of your dick skin was cleaved off or not. *Ouch!* But, in the twenty-first

> Using the writings of the Apostle Paul outside of the original historical context in order to create *any division* in the body of Christ is not only anachronistic and illogical, but ethically out of line.

century, we could include the modern sociological dividing line of "gay" and "straight," to which I'd have to guess Paul would emphatically rebuke as part of a false gospel that inevitably only leads to death (Gal 1:6, 2:19). Admittedly, this is speculative, but given the context of Paul's letters to the Romans and Galatians, it seems right in line with how he viewed inclusivity and unity in the Church.[16]

In Closing

At the end of the day, what matters most—especially for those who profess trust in Jesus Christ—is how we love. The writer of 1 John teaches us that "God is love" (1 John 4:8). Paul sums up the entire law in one sentence: "You shall love your neighbor as yourself" (Gal 5:14). Jesus himself teaches us that the greatest commandment is to love God and our neighbor as our self (Matt 22:36–40; Mark 12:30–31), and that in order to be his disciple, we must "have love for one another" (John 13:35). *This obviously includes those in the GSM community!*

So, do a thought experiment for me. Imagine you are a married, heterosexual person, and imagine your life up to this point altered in only one way, that instead of partnering with someone of the opposite sex, you had partnered with someone of the same sex. All of your shared experiences are the same. All of your loving moments are the same. All of your times of joy, hope, even suffering, alike in every way save for one. How, then, would it be *sinful*—rather than *loving*—if the only variable is that you are sharing these experiences with someone who shares your gender or sexual orientation? How, exactly, would you be violating what Jesus calls the greatest commandment, that we are to love God and neighbor?

Questions like these should give us great pause. Once upon a time they forced me to stop and reflect. And when I did, I could no longer stand justified in front of my God and my neighbor in telling any two consenting adults that they couldn't share their lives together in the same way I was sharing my life with my lovely wife. So, I repented—that is, I changed my mind—and started practicing how to love my GSM family in the same way Christ Jesus loves them; starting by openly welcoming them into the blessed community that has no dividing lines whatsoever.

6

Indeed Very Many: Universalism in the Early Church

"Strictly historically speaking, any universalism is heresy—according to all major branches of Christianity."[1]

—ROGER OLSON

"That position [Universalism] has consistently been held as heretical by the Church for two-thousand years...You can go back to Athanasius, you can go back to Augustine, you can go back to Huss, and Tyndale, and others"[2]

—MARK DRISCOLL

While the doctrine of universal reconciliation has indeed been a minority position throughout *most* of Christian history—albeit not quite two-thousand years—all one has to do is turn to Augustine, a clear non-Universalist, to see how it was once upon a time a rather popular doctrine. He, in the fifth century, rather dismissively writes:

> It is quite in vain, then, that some—*indeed very many*—yield to merely human feelings and deplore the notion of the eternal punishment of the damned and their interminable and

> When Augustine described the Universalists as "indeed very many" (*immo quam plurimi*), in truth, what he meant is that they were a "vast majority."

perpetual misery. They do not believe that such things will be. Not that they would go counter to divine Scripture—but, yielding to their own human feelings, they soften what seems harsh and give a milder emphasis to statements they believe are meant more to terrify than to express literal truth (emphasis mine).[3]

When Augustine described the Universalists as "indeed very many" (*immo quam plurimi*), in truth, what he meant is that they were a "vast majority."[4] That is what the Latin word *plurimi*, from the adjective *plurimus*, implies. And though Augustine himself didn't affirm this doctrine (although he may have in the beginning[5]), he at least recognized that Universalism, or in other words the "theory of apokatastasis,"[6] was quite an influential doctrine in his day and the centuries that preceded him.

A quick snapshot of the most influential early Christian Universalists, from Patristics scholar Ilaria Ramelli, certainly reinforces Augustine's admission:

> The main Patristic supporters of the apokatastasis theory, such as Bardaisan, Clement, Origen, Didymus, St. Anthony, St. Pamphilus Martyr, Methodius, St. Macrina, St. Gregory of Nyssa (and probably the two other Cappadocians), St. Evagrius Ponticus, Diodore of Tarsus, Theodore of Mopsuestia, St. John of Jerusalem, Rufinus, St. Jerome and St. Augustine (at least initially)…Cassian, St. Issac of Nineveh, St. John of Dalyatha, Ps. Dionysius the Areopagite, probably St. Maximus the Confessor,

up to John the Scot Eriugena, and many others, grounded their Christian doctrine of apokatastasis first of all in the Bible.[7]

A list this impressive forces us to ask two questions.

First, was it merely a yielding to human feelings that caused "indeed very many" to "deplore the notion of the eternal punishment of the damned," as Augustine suggests, or was it something else? Given the scholarship of the above list, it seems an unfair charge to levy against the Universalists. And while Augustine—or any of the other infernalists or annihilationists for that matter—is not obliged to agree with them, their collective credentials certainly earns them, at the very least, a seat at the theological discussion table.

The second question that immediately pops into my mind is this: Has Universalism *really* been considered heretical by the Christian Church for her entire two-thousand-year history, as Mark Driscoll so emphatically states?

The simple truth is that Driscoll is not correct to suggest that Universalism has been heretical throughout the entirety of Christendom. Far from it, in fact, since the theory of apokatastasis wasn't declared heretical until the sixth century, first by Justinian (a despotic Byzantine emperor) and then at the Fifth Ecumenical Council of Constantinople. And even then, it wasn't so much the eschatological conclusions of St. Origen, Clement of Alexandria, and other Universalists that was the cause of such doctrinal controversy, it was, as historian Morwenna Ludlow points out, Origen's ideas about "the pre-existence of souls, their 'fall' into human bodies, and a spiritual resurrection."[8] To put it plainly, universal reconciliation was unfairly condemned because it was connected with these other contentious ideas.

Furthermore, neither the Apostles' and Nicene Creeds—which were written a few hundred years prior to the two aforementioned councils—fail to preclude the possibility of the "restoration of all things" mentioned by the writer of Luke-Acts (Acts 3:21). The earliest Greek version of the Apostles' Creed, for example, reads as follows:

> I believe in God the Father Almighty and in Jesus Christ his only son our Lord, who was by the Holy Ghost, born of the Virgin Mary, suffered under Pontius Pilate, was crucified and buried. The third day he arose again from the dead; he ascended into heaven and sitteth at the right hand of the Father. I believe in the Holy Ghost, the Holy Church, the forgiveness of sins; the resurrection of the body. Amen.[9]

The later Nicene Creed is not much different (although, in order to push back against the heretical teachings of Arius, it *does* add emphasis on the Son and Father being "of one substance"). Nevertheless, nothing in it precludes the possibility that all will be saved. It is not until the Athanasian Creed, in 500 CE, where the phrase "they that have done evil, into everlasting fire" is introduced in creedal form.

So, I must ask: if the possibility of eternal hellfire and damnation was such a looming threat, why was there no mention of it in the earliest Greek creedal statements? Why wasn't the theory of apokatastasis put to rest early on, if the Bible was so clear? In Irenaeus' lengthy second-century book entitled *Against Heresies*, for example, why wasn't Universalism included? Why weren't theologians like Origen, Clement, and Gregory of Nyssa—the final editor of the Nicene Creed for goodness' sake—condemned outright for their belief in universal reconciliation? And how could they even come to such conclusions if true Church doctrine, ripe with hellfire, is as clear as Driscoll and so many others would attempt to have us believe? Was it simply a matter of them yielding to human feelings, as Augustine puts it? Was it something else, something malicious perhaps? Or, lo and behold, were they actually on to something, and therefore, should be paid attention to more closely than they are at present?

Obviously, I *do* believe that they were in fact "on to something" and therefore should be afforded more of our collective attention. One of the primary reasons, although certainly not the only one, can be boiled down to a matter of language.

Let me explain.

Whereas "hellfire" theologians like Augustine primarily spoke Latin, folks like Origen, Clement, and later, Gregory of Nyssa, spoke Greek. This is important because it means there is a direct linguistic and even philosophical path from the Greek New Testament—heavily influenced by the Apostle Paul—to these earliest theologians. Historian J.W. Hanson reminds us:

> The greatest of all Christian apologists and exegetes, and the first man in Christendom since Paul, was a distinct Universalist. He [Origen] could not have misunderstood or misrepresented the teachings of his Master. The language of the New Testament was his mother tongue. He derived the teachings of Christ from Christ himself in a direct line through his teacher Clement; and he placed the defense of Christianity on Universalist grounds.[10]

In contrast, the same cannot be said of Augustine. He despised the Greek language.[11] In fact, he went so far as to say that while he loved Latin, he out and out *hated* Greek.[12] And so, compared to his Greek-speaking predecessors, when it came to translating or interpreting New Testament Greek, Augustine was a bit out of his league and indeed made some vital errors. Hanson makes the following point:

> It is anomalous in the history of criticism that generations of scholars should take their cue in a matter of Greek definition from one who admits that he had "learned almost nothing of Greek," and was "not competent to read and understand" the language, and reject the position held by those who were born Greeks! That such a man should contradict and subvert the teachings of such men as Clement, Origen, the Gregories and others whose mother-tongue was Greek, is passing strange.[13]

For an example, let's take a look at Matthew 25:46. The passage reads: "And these will go away into eternal punishment [*aionios kolasis*], but the righteous into eternal life [*aionios zoe*]." On the surface, it seems clear: some are punished forever and some live forever. But, as Hanson points out in the following, this interpretation, in part, stems from Augustine's erroneous linguistic presuppositions. He writes: "Augustine assumed and insisted that the words defining the duration of punishment, in the New Testament, teach its endlessness, and the claim set up by Augustine is the one still held by advocates of 'the dying belief,' that *aeternus* in the Latin, and *aionios* in the original Greek, mean interminable duration."[14] But is this true? Is it true that *aeternus* and *aionios* are synonymous, and that both have a quantitative meaning of time-everlasting? Well, no, according to the Greek-speaking biblical scholar William Barclay:

To take the word *aionios*, when it refers to blessings and punishment, to mean lasting forever is to oversimplify, and indeed to misunderstand, the word altogether. It means far more than that. It means that that which the faithful will receive and that which the unfaithful will suffer is that which it befits God's nature and character to bestow and to inflict—and beyond that we who are men cannot go, except to remember that that nature and character are holy love.[15]

New Testament scholar Christopher Marshall drives the same point home:

> The word "eternal" is used in both a qualitative and a quantitative sense in the Bible. It is sometimes urged that if eternal life in Matthew 25:46 is everlasting in duration, so too must be eternal punishment. But "eternal" in both phrases may simply designate that the realities in question pertain to the future age. Furthermore, inasmuch as life, by definition, is an ongoing state, "eternal life" includes the idea of everlasting existence. But punishment is a process rather than a state, and elsewhere when "eternal" describes an act or process, it is the consequences rather than the process that are everlasting (e.g. Heb 6:2, "eternal judgment"; Heb 9:12, "eternal redemption"; Mark 3:29, "eternal sin"; 2 Thess 1:9, "eternal destruction"; Jude 7, "eternal fire"). Eternal punishment is therefore something that is ultimate in significance and everlasting in effect, not in duration.[16]

So, in other words, to think of *aionios* in a *strictly* quantitative manner—in the same way one may think of the Latin "equivalent" *aeternus*—rather than also qualitatively (i.e., in the context of God's eternal loving nature), would be to set one's self up to make a fatal error. And the Western Church, with Augustine (and even Tertullian before him) at the forefront, has made this fatal error, which has then led to a misunderstanding of the vitally important doctrine of God's posthumous restorative chastisement (*aionios kolasis*).

None of this is to diminish what Augustine has done for the church, or to say that he wasn't a brilliant theologian. He was! But Christian theology didn't begin with him nor is he the ultimate authority on what "sound doctrine" looks like. Gregory of Nyssa, the "Augustine of the East," for example, had much to say about "sound doctrine," including his vision for the ultimate fate of humanity. So too did Origen, and Clement, and Theodoret the Blessed, and the whole host of others—*indeed very many*! I'll leave you with a few of their juiciest quotes so you can see with your own eyes what I am talking about:[17]

- "For it is evident that God will in truth be all in all when there shall be no evil in existence, when every created being is at harmony with itself and every tongue shall confess that Jesus Christ is Lord; when every creature shall have been made one body." —Gregory of Nyssa

- "So then, when the end has been restored to the beginning, and the termination of things compared with their commencement, that condition of things will be re-established in which rational nature was placed, when it had no need to eat of the tree of the knowledge of good and evil; so that when all feeling of wickedness has been removed, and the individual has been purified and cleansed, he who alone is the one good God becomes to him 'all,' and that not in the case of a few individuals, or of a considerable number, but he himself is 'all in all.' And when death shall no longer anywhere exist, nor the sting of death, nor any evil at all, then verily God will be 'all in all.'" —Origen of Alexandria

- "All men [humans] are Christ's, some by knowing him, the rest not yet. He is the Savior, not of some and the rest not. For how is he Savior and Lord, if not Savior and Lord of all?" —Clement of Alexandria

- "In the present life God is in all, for his nature is without limits, but he is not *all* in all. But in the coming life, when mortality is at an end and immortality granted, and sin has no longer any place, God will be all in all. For the Lord, who loves man, punishes medicinally, that he may check the course of impiety." —Theodoret the Blessed

It's a pity we tend to write theologians like these out of the history books; and a pity our Christian leaders either fail to recognize this, or fail to accurately report it. And while none of them should be presumed to be correct, they also shouldn't be ignored and denounced. The Church deserves better. She deserves an accurate and robust historical snapshot, not one papered over by half-truths and out and out lies.

7
The Cross of Christ: Pulling a Sacrificial One-Eighty

"The wrath of God is due to the legal requirements of punishing the sinner. Remember, the sinner is someone who has broken the law of God, hence, the legality of punishment; and since Jesus is our propitiation and turns away the lawful wrath of God, we have further evidence that Christ's sacrifice was to avert God's righteous wrath against us, the sinners."[1]

—MATT SLICK

"Is there more than one thing to say about the atonement? Absolutely. Are there a variety of implications and applications that can be drawn from the cross of Christ? Of course. But none of them make sense if Christ did not die in our place to assuage the wrath of God. Penal substitution is not a theory—one suggested idea that may or may not be true. Penal substitutionary atonement is the hope of sinners, the heart of the gospel, and the good news without which all other news regarding the cross is null and void."[2]

—KEVIN DEYOUNG

In the West, the cross of Christ is primarily thought of in one way and one way only. Over the details we may quibble, but we are often told that Jesus died in order to save sinners from the wrath of God. In other words, he was a substitutionary sacrifice—he died in our place—to appease the Father's justice, honor, and wrath. The story of how we get to such a place basically goes like this:

> God created humankind in his image and saw that it was good. Then, humanity sinned and experienced a "fall." This created a huge problem, one that finite creatures simply could not make up for. Why? Because God's justice and honor are such that only a payment of infinite proportions could make atonement. So, God, in his infinite wisdom, sent himself in the form of a Son—one truly human—in order to be sacrificed to himself so that his justice and honor could be upheld. Thus, he fulfills the conundrum of needing an infinite payment from finite humans. Now, those who accept the blood sacrifice could be forgiven their sins. The rest? The wrath of the infinite Father forever abides on them.

I understand the propensity to mock and scorn such a view. "New atheists" in particular have a field day with it. However, we are not going to take part in the mockery here (as much as I would like to). It probably wouldn't be all that helpful though. What we *are* going to do is simply touch on some of the initial problems this view of the atonement creates so that, in the following section, we can introduce some healthier—as well as more orthodox—views of how the Cross saves us, and what, exactly, it saves us from (hint: it's not God!)

Penal Substitutionary Atonement (PSA) and its Inherent Problems

PROBLEM I: THE DEBT-COLLECTING GOD

The first issue this view creates is that it basically depicts God as a debt collector. A debt was accrued and payment has to be made in order for the Father's forgiveness and mercy to flow forth into the world. Contrary to the Pauline claim that love keeps no record of wrongs (1 Cor 13:5), the sins that are stockpiled are kept on the books until the spilt blood of Jesus covers them. Then, and only then, is the debt paid. And so, then and only then can the wrongs be taken off the books.

PROBLEM II: THE RETRIBUTIVE GOD

The second issue is the way in which original sin gets interpreted by folks in the PSA camp. Indeed, their understanding of humanity's fall exposes God as a retributive punisher. What I mean is that our sin is just so damn disgusting that God must have retribution in order to be appeased. To that end, the punishment Jesus took was the punishment we deserve. The lashings, the flogging, the mocking, all of it something God would do to us or have done to us if Jesus hadn't taken the beating for us. That, or something similar. Those of us who accept the transaction are spared. Those that don't get their just desserts in the end—infinitely re-*tributed* for their finite sins.

PROBLEM III: THE ARCHAIC-MINDED GOD

If history has taught us anything, it is that the gods we create demand blood sacrifices in order for their wrath to be appeased. Girard has helped elucidate this more so than anyone. Think of all the virgins that were thrown into volcanoes throughout the eons. The issue is that the penal substitutionary model of the atonement paints the Father in a similar light; the only difference being that God is both the one demanding the sacrifice *and* the sacrifice itself. So, while it is not surprising that we would sort of see Jesus as the "virgin we throw into a volcano to appease an angry god," it *is* rather ironic, especially given that our Jewish forefathers had already taken humanity *away from* such a view of "at-one-ment." As James Alison reminds us:

> The Jewish priestly rite was already [...] way ahead of the "Aztec" version we attribute to it. Even at that time [pre-exilic], it was understood that it was not about humans trying desperately to satisfy God, but God taking the initiative of breaking through towards us. In other words, atonement was something of which we were the *beneficiaries*.[3]

PROBLEM IV: THE JANUS-FACED GOD

A fourth issue we run into with this view is that two manifestations of the Trinity are pitted against one another. In one corner, you have the wrath of God, which needs the shedding of blood in order to forgive sins (Heb 9:22). In the other corner, you have Jesus, who forgave freely (Matt 9:2; 18:22; Luke 23:34; John 8:11; 20:19–23). In other words, Jesus forgave even though blood hadn't been spilled. One major issue with this is that the New Testament is fairly clear that both the Father and the Son are, in nature, eternally the same (Matt 11:27; John 1:18; 4:34; 5:19–20; 6:38, 46; 8:28; 10:29; 12:49; Col 2:9; Heb 13:8). In later creedal formulations, it is said that they are *homoousios*, or "of one substance."[4] To put it simply, then, Jesus reveals what the Father is like and what he has always been like. Yet, in this particular model, that hardly seems so.

PROBLEM V: THE UNFOLLOWABLE GOD

When the Father and the Son are pitted against each other, choosing the correct one to follow becomes quite a conundrum. If we forgive like Jesus, for example, then forgiveness will precede repentance (Matt 9:2; 18:22; Luke 23:34; John 8:11; 20:19–23). However, if we choose to forgive like the Father, we will only forgive those that show repentance, or after they make a payment of some kind.[5] But did Jesus not command that we are to be perfect as our heavenly Father (Matt 5:48)?

> It seems rather dubious, then, if the way in which the Son and Father forgive is as dissimilar as East is from the West.

And is that perfection not displayed as pure mercy (Luke 6:36)? It seems rather dubious, then, if the way in which the Son and Father forgive is as dissimilar as East is from the West.

Introducing Two Alternatives

Over the course of its history, Christianity has put forth alternatives to the penal substitutionary view. In fact, many theories predate PSA (a theory not even formalized until John Calvin, a lawyer, put it together during the Reformation. Essentially, with some slight alterations, it's just like Anselm's eleventh-century "Satisfaction Theory," which posits that Christ died in order to satisfy God's honor.[6] Calvin took *that* idea and emphasized God's wrath rather than his honor.)

So, if this way of thinking about the atonement has not always been the norm, what *were* Christian theologians saying about the cross prior to the Middle Ages? Interestingly, something much different than we commonly hear today. In the following section, we'll touch on two themes, and then expand upon these initial thoughts. Our hope will be to provide a robust atonement theology, one void of an economy of exchange in which the Father needs the blood of the Son in order for his mercy to flow into the creation.

MORAL INFLUENCE

From the beginning, Christians have talked about the life and death of Christ as a model for our own lives. Clement of Alexandria (150–215 CE) was one of these:

> For [Christ] came down, for this he assumed human nature, for this he willingly endured the sufferings of humanity, that he being reduced to the measure of our weakness, he might raise us to the measure of his power. And just before he poured out his offering, when he gave himself as ransom, he left us a new testament: "I give you my love." What is the nature and extent of this love? For each of us he laid down his life, the life which was worth the whole universe, and he requires in return that we should do the same for each other.[7]

Later, however, Christ's moral influence would be broadened into a way of talking about atonement more specifically. (Peter Abelard, a twelfth-century French theologian, is the one who gets credit for the development of the theory.) And, while it has its strengths, both biblically and ethically, it suffers only in that it simply doesn't say enough about what happened in the life and death of Jesus. In other words, while the theory isn't necessarily wrong—that is, Jesus Christ *is* the model of what it means to be "at-one" with the Father (John 5:19–20; 6:38; 8:28; 10:29; 12:49)—it leaves us wanting a more robust explanation as to how Jesus, and most specifically, the cross, saves us.

CHRISTUS VICTOR

That is where *Christus Victor* can help lend a hand. In *A Journey with Two Mystics*, my best friend, Michael Machuga, sums up the theory with this beautiful catena of Scripture:

> Satan has enslaved humanity with the fear of death (Heb 2:14–15). All manners of evil arise from this bondage. But Christ comes to set humanity free from Satan's power, that is, "to destroy the devil's work" (1 Pet 5:8). He does so by enduring the cross and by then being raised to life by God (Acts 2:23–25). In doing so, Christ "disarmed the rulers and authorities, exposing them to public disgrace by leading them in a triumphal parade" (Col 2:15). Christ is made Lord (Rom 14:11; Phil 2:11), given the Name above all names (Phil 2:9), and will reign until death, the last enemy, is destroyed (1 Cor 15:24–26). Death will then be cast into the lake of fire (Rev 20:10, 14) so that "God may be all in all" (1 Cor 15:28).[8]

Needless to say, an atonement theology such as this takes us much further than "moral influence." Here, Christ is indeed our model for "moral living," but he's much more than that. *Christus Victor* proclaims that because of him, everything that stands in our way from being "at-one" with God has been defeated, including *sin* and *death*. And, excitingly, we can apply it in such a way that doesn't necessitate a "traditionally sacrificial" interpretation of the cross, while at the same time taking sin seriously (an charge PSA folks tend to make against their non-PSA interlocutors).

In the following section, we are going to unpack what this may mean for us. Our goal, most specifically, will be to answer the question: How, exactly, does Christ's death save us from "sin" and "death?"

The Victory of Christ

DEATH IS PUT TO DEATH

Clearly, death is a problem. Allow me to rephrase. According to the writer of Hebrews, it is *the* problem: "So that through death he might destroy the one who has the power of death, that is, the devil, and free those who all their lives were held in *slavery* by the *fear of death*" (Heb 2:14–15, emphasis mine). The writer of 1 John also emphasizes that "The Son of God was revealed for this purpose, to destroy the works of the devil" (1 John 3:8). Put these together, and we can easily say that humanity's greatest problem is that the devil and his works have enslaved humanity through the fear of death.

Incidentally, this fear of death is what cultural anthropologist Ernest Becker posited is the primary source of human-initiated suffering. That is to say, the neurosis death brings is the underlying cause of most of our violence (i.e., sin). What happens is that because we can think abstractly about our own death, we build these so-called "hero systems"—cultures, religions, political ideologies, and so on—that must be defended against all alternative systems. Psychologist Richard Beck explains how this mechanism works, and why it's such a problem:

> In short, alternative hero systems—other values, worldviews, and ways of life—threaten to undo everything that has made our lives feel significant, meaningful, and secure in the face of death. The ideological Other—usually some out-group member who has different values and beliefs from our own—presents us with an implicit critique of our personal hero system. This threatens us to the core, attacks the very source of our self-esteem. This means that the ideological Other—the out-group member who is simply different from us—doesn't really have to do anything particularly threatening. His or her mere existence is enough to menace us. Outgroup members represent, on the edges of our awareness, a dissenting voice that suggest that the way we've constructed our identities and the criteria we've used to manage our self-esteem are not eternal and transcendent but are instead arbitrary human fictions.
>
> So, what do we do in the face of that threat? Simply stated, we demonize these people. Rather than endure existential discomfort, it's easier to double down on our worldview and to see those different from us as malevolent agents. We aggress against these "others." In mild forms, we view them as confused or mistaken. More severely, they grow to become enemies we have to forcibly eliminate.[9]

All we have to do to see this play out in real-time is open our eyes. Look around and you will constantly see shots fired at one another. Not only do the Christians fight the Muslims (and vice-versa), but the Catholics fight the Protestants, and Protestants demonize the Anabaptists; Sunnis attack the Shias, and both go after the Sufis. More "secularly-speaking," Capitalists demonize Socialists, while Socialists blame Capitalists for the world's problems; but "New Atheists" know better and point to religion and its adherents as the true cause. And on and on it goes.

Regardless of who's to blame, the answer to this dilemma, according to the earliest Christians, is in the person of Christ Jesus, who conquered death and the fear it brings. What *Christus Victor* emphasizes is that because of Christ's death and subsequent resurrection, he triumphed over, among other things, not only the fear of death, but death itself. He died and went to Hades, conquered it, and now holds the keys (Rev 1:18). Whereas the devil once had the power to wield death as a way to keep humanity in bondage, Christ now has that power. But, with that power, he does the opposite of the devil; he comes to us, in all our confusion and misery, to show us that new life awaits us. He shatters our fear of death by showing us his hands and his side, and by forgiving us "while we were yet sinners" (Rom 5:8; John 20:19–20).

This is how we are saved from the bondage that our fear of death holds us under. By affirming the Resurrection—and as such, our own future resurrection—we open up new possibilities for our love to flow forth in the present. In other words, because we have nothing to hold onto any longer—now that the sting of death has been taken away—we are free to give ourselves in love for the other (the Greek term for this is *kenosis*). As the writer of 1 John tells us: "We know that we have passed from death to life because we love one another" (1 John 3:14). To put it in the simplest way I can, the dynamic duo of fear and death are undone by an even more dynamic duo: Love and Resurrection.[10]

> The sacrifice of Jesus is not to be thought of as something that changes God and his mind, it is something that God does through Jesus that changes us and our ways of thinking.

THE SUBVERSION OF SACRIFICE

A second major problem Christ's death saves us from is this business of sacrificing to the gods. For as long as humans have been around, we have been engaging in this practice. The greatest of the sacrifices have always been the purest: firstborn sons, virgin daughters, unblemished lambs, and so on. And while the penal substitutionary theory of the atonement keeps in line with this sacrificial thinking—the virgin Son is sacrificed to appease the wrath of the Father—the true message of the New Testament actually seems to be quite the opposite. In other words, the sacrifice of Jesus is not to be thought of as something that changes God and his mind, it is something that God does through Jesus that changes us and our ways of thinking. Thus, it saves us.

So, how exactly does God do this?

In two ways.

First, notice how the New Testament message flips the common way of sacrificial thinking on its head: *God* puts forth the Lamb, *we* receive him, yet *God* raises him up again. To put it this way, God offers the sacrifice to humans who cannot help but do what they do best. Yet God also gets the last word—the word of life. The writer of Acts repeatedly makes this point:

- Acts 2:23–24: "This man...you crucified...but God raised him up."

- Acts 3:15: "You killed the Author of life, whom God raised from the dead."

- Acts 4:10: "Jesus Christ of Nazareth, whom you crucified, whom God raised from the dead."

In doing this, we are shown two things at the same time: what God is truly like and, consequently, what we are like. What I mean is that when the Father puts forth the Son (and, also, when he raises him up), it is to show how the whole sacrificial system is not something he desires, for he never desires death (Ezek 33:11). Rather, we do. I love how the writer of Hebrews drives home this very point:

> Indeed, *under the law* almost everything is purified with blood, and without the shedding of blood there is no forgiveness of sins...[however] when, Christ came into the world, he said, "*Sacrifices and offerings you have not desired*, but a body you have prepared for me; in burnt offerings and sin offerings you have taken no pleasure. Then I said, 'See, God, I have come to do your will, O God' (in the scroll of the book it is written of me)." When he said above, "You have neither desired nor taken

pleasure in sacrifices and offerings and burnt offerings and sin offerings" (these are offered according to the law), then he added, "See, I have come to do your will." (Heb 9:22; 10:5–8, emphasis mine)

Notice the contrast: *sacrifice* and *doing God's will*. On the one hand, the desire for sacrifice, while historically something we can't help but project onto the entire pantheon of gods, is shown to be purely a human desire: "These are offered according to the law." On the other hand, the one who perfectly does God's will is the one who allows this law-based system to fall onto him while forgiving it all. Hence, Jesus shows us how the Father, rather than being just another god who demands sacrifice, is actually the one true God who becomes the sacrifice on our behalf. That is what we mean by "Christ died *for* us." (Rom 4:25; 8:32) He dies for our benefit. Why? To expose the system for what it is—a system predicated on more and more blood and death (Luke 11:49–51)—while yet showing pure grace in the face of it.

> Jesus shows us how the Father, rather than being just another god who demands sacrifice, is actually the one true God who becomes the sacrifice on our behalf.

The second point I want to make is that God takes humanity's practice of ritualistic sacrifice and gives us a new ritual: the Eucharist. As Robert Hamerton-Kelly points out in *The Gospel and the Sacred*, pretty much everything Jesus does during the Last Supper is subversive in nature:

> The institution of the Eucharist is an inversion of the temple sacrifices. The usual direction of the sacrificial offering

is reversed; instead of the worshiper giving to the god, the god is giving to the worshiper. Jesus "gives" (*didomi*) his body and blood, symbolized by bread and wine, to them instead of their giving their bodies and blood, symbolized by money, to the temple. Just as money symbolizes life given to the temple, so bread and wine symbolize the divine life given to the worshiper. Bruce Chilton suggests plausibly that the words of institution, "This is my body…this is my blood" (Mark 14:22–24) intend to present the breaking of the bread and the pouring of the wine as substitutes for the killing of victims in the temple. The room substitutes for the temple, the table for the altar, and the sharing of food for the killing of the victim. Normally, the worshiper brings the offering into sacred space; here, the upper room is the nonsacred counterpart of the holy of holies, and so the offering is made outside of sacred space. Thus, the sacrificial system is subverted by the reversal of the direction of its ritual logic.[11]

The beautiful thing about this whole event is that Jesus doesn't simply tell his disciples what *not* to do, he gives us something *to do*. We are ritualistic creatures, after all, and as such, need rituals in order to get along in life. But these rituals, as we discussed in chapter 3, demand blood. They demand victims.

> **This new ritual that leads to new community centers on a table, not an altar. It centers on bread and wine, not bodies and blood.**

Not the Eucharist, however. This new ritual that leads to new community centers on a table, not an altar. It centers on bread and wine, not bodies and blood. It centers, even, on sharing this meal with one's enemies. Remember, even Judas—the man Jesus knew would betray him—was present and had his feet washed by the Lord (John 13:1–5). Such is the radical inclusivity of the Eucharistic meal.

In Closing

At the end of the day, what matters most when it comes to atonement is whether we hold to a healing doctrine or not. Does our atonement theory bring peace or not? What I have discovered is that, while the nonviolent atonement theology I now affirm has done just that, my former views, ripe with penal language, never did. In fact, penal substitutionary atonement theory did just the opposite; it caused me great grief and confusion. For a time, it even played its part in driving me to atheism (and I know I'm not the only one).

That said, could PSA still be the most correct understanding of the Cross? Sure. One can find substitutionary language all throughout the Scriptures. One can read about God's wrath and judicial nature as well. This cannot be disputed. But, what *can* be disputed is whether the sacrifice of Jesus is something that changes God's mind about us, or whether it is to change our minds about God. To ask it this way: Does the cross save us from God *or* from something else (e.g. the Principalities and Powers, the practice of sacrifice, the fear of death, the devil, sin, and so on)? Throughout this chapter, I hope I did my job in showing that those who affirm the latter should be afforded a seat at the table with the majority of Western Christians who conclude the former; that we can offer some critique and pushback against their idea that, on the cross, the wrath of God was being poured out on a broken and bloody Jesus. A greater hope is that I did a bit more than that; namely that I put forth an understanding of the cross that actually subverts the "traditional" violent one that has troubled so many Christians and non-Christians alike.

8
Locked from the Inside? Predestination, Free Will, and the Doctrine of Hell

"There are only two kinds of people in the end: those who say to God, 'Thy will be done,' and those to whom God says, in the end, 'Thy will be done.' All that are in hell, choose it."[1]

—C.S. LEWIS

"God will allow some people to be deceived and make an irrational decision for damnation."[2]

—JOHN SANDERS

"As God hath appointed the elect unto glory, so hath he, by the eternal and most free purpose of his will, foreordained all the means thereunto. Wherefore, they who are elected...are effectually called unto faith in Christ by his Spirit working in due season, are justified, adopted, sanctified, and kept by his power, through faith, unto salvation. Neither are any other redeemed by Christ, effectually called, justified, adopted, sanctified, and saved, but the elect only.

The rest of mankind God was pleased, according to the unsearchable counsel of his own will, whereby he extendeth or withholdeth

mercy, as he pleases, for the glory of his sovereign power over his creatures, to pass by; and to ordain them to dishonor and wrath for their sin, to the praise of his glorious justice."
—WESTMINSTER CONFESSION OF FAITH, CH. III, ARTICLES VI AND VII

When Christian infernalists think of the doctrine of hell, and specifically how one may find themselves consigned there, they generally do so in one of two ways. Some, following in the footsteps of Augustine and later, Calvin, suggest that God sends folks to hell for their sin while others, loosely following Arminius or even perhaps Pelagius, argue that sinners send themselves there through their own free will. As C.S. Lewis so famously put it: "The gates of hell are locked from the inside."[3] And, while we could quibble over these details, nuancing them hither and yon as some are wont to do, for our purposes, these rough outlines will have to suffice.

Now, because I don't subscribe to either infernalist position, it will be my task to put forth an alternative. Before that happens though, we need to take a look at some of the initial problems each view presents. Then and only then can we begin to see how a third option—one void of eternal suffering of any kind—begins to shine through as the most cogent way of understanding humanity's freedom and how it relates to our ultimate fate.

The Problem with the Augustinian/Calvinist View

If the Bible indeed argues for "difficult truths" about the Universe, as I've so often heard, the Augustinian doctrine of hell is the difficult truth *par excellence*. Augustinians posit that while sinners in fact make choices that lead to damnation, it is God, first and foremost, who is ultimately responsible for such a fate. Simply put, God capriciously chooses whom he will save and, subsequently, whom he will damn on the sheer basis that he is free to do so. As Augustine argued in *Confessions,* God's sovereign grace is defined thus:

> "To act beyond any external necessity whatsoever"—to act in love beyond human control or understanding; to act in creation, judgment, and redemption; to *freely* give the Son of God and the Spirit of God for salvation, empowerment, and guidance; and "to shape the destinies of all creation and the ends of the two human societies, the 'city of earth' and the 'city of God.'"[4]

As time passes, this idea of "divine sovereignty" gets taken one step further. As John Calvin would later argue, God is even said to sovereignly engage in what we would likely call evil: "Thieves, murderers, and other evildoers, are instruments of divine providence, being employed by the Lord himself to execute the judgments which he has resolved to inflict."[5] Not to be crass, and perhaps I'm misreading things here, but this seems to suggest men who rape little boys and girls, for example, are instruments of God's providence. Or, when ISIS beheads a whole slew of innocent women and children, they are doing so in order to "execute the judgments which [God] has resolved to inflict."[6] And yes, that even means once God—through Hitler—got done burning the Jews alive in ghastly torture chambers, they were then sent to a similar, albeit vastly worse, place by the Father (assuming they died without Jesus as their savior). All according to his divine, sovereign will.

Given the fact that one would be hard pressed to call these things "good," I am forced to ask: "If language has any meaning at all, how can *this God* be called good?"

"Well, hold on now Matthew," one may rebut: "You are forgetting that humanity experienced a fall, and subsequently, have inherited the guilt of Adam, as it were. So, we are, in the eyes of God, now but 'filthy rags,' wretches that don't even deserve an ounce of grace and mercy. In fact, we not only *justly* deserve death, but an eternal life of suffering, completely separated from God."

> Not only does it seem passing strange to suggest guilt can be inherited, beyond that, it seems morally dubious.

Statements like these, however biblically justified, just spin us in circles. Not only does it seem passing strange to suggest guilt can be inherited, beyond that, it seems morally dubious. Orthodox theologian David Bentley Hart takes it even one step further:

> The very idea of an "inherited guilt" is a logical absurdity, rather on the order of a "square circle;" all the doctrine truly asserts is that God imputes to innocent creatures a guilt they can never have contracted, out of what from any sane perspective can only be called malice. But this is just the beginning of the problem. For one broad venerable stream of tradition, God on the basis of this imputation delivers the vast majority of the race to perpetual torment, including infants who die unbaptized.[7]

Nevertheless, *if* inherited guilt and the consignment to eternal damnation that stems from it is indeed true, as the Augustinians suggest, have we not reinforced our initial concerns that language has to be reduced to meaninglessness in order for this to be true? For, again I ask: "How can *this God* be called good?"

For some, like the medieval voluntarists, the solution is simply to argue that God isn't bound by goodness, as we may define goodness, but that whatever God does is good simply because he does it. For these folks, God *could* impute people with "inherited guilt" and send them to eternal hell—in spite of the fact that if he desired to, he *could* save them—and it would still be considered "good" simply because God did it. *Heck!* God could act however God wants—he could rape, maim, torture, psychologically abuse, and laugh all-the-while—and because he was doing it, that would be the benchmark for what is to be considered "goodness." To that end, we must then conclude that what *we* call "goodness," or "mercy," or "justice," or "grace," or "love," may in fact be the opposite to what God means by these things, and we may never really know. And if this is true, then haven't we arrived at a place where, as Hart notices, faith and nihilism are essentially the same thing?[8] In our book, *A Journey with Two Mystics*, my best friend and comrade in life, Michael Machuga, puts it this way:

> It is impossible to escape our humanity and the terms that we use to describe the world around us. So, if God has a different working definition of justice [or; "goodness," "mercy," "grace," "love"] than we do, that is, if his justice is separate from his goodness, or if he values retribution over restoration, and we have no access to this—experiential or otherwise—then there is not much we can do about it...The best we can say is that, as per our definition, God is acting unjustly. Perhaps he would say the same of us! Either way, we would seem to be at an impasse.[9]

Do we see the glaring issues here?

Yet, this is hardly the worst consequence of such fucking absurdities. No! The biggest problem lies in the imposed psychological horror such a view leads to. In this theological system, God cannot be fully trusted, and, as such, a person can never know if they are saved. They can never "relax into the arms of God," as James Alison may put it. Sure, a person can look at their life, see the fruit of their faith, and *think* they are saved. They can do as Reformed thinker William Perkins did in his following syllogism:

1. Only those who repent and believe are the children of God.

2. I am a repenting person.

3. Therefore, I am a child of God.[10]

Yet, ultimately, this is an exercise in futility because when looking at their own repentance, it could all be a façade. They may in fact think and believe they are among "the elect," but in the end, the rug may be pulled out from under them, revealing them to be elected for nothing but eternal damnation.[11] Why? This little Calvinist tenet called "the perseverance of the saints." In other words, those elected for eternal life must persevere in the faith until the end, and since that hasn't come to pass yet, one can really never know if this will occur. And then what? Off they go, into the fire that was kindled long before they were even born!

Augustinians know this! And while some, like Calvinist blogger Michael Patton, are okay with it, others go mad thinking about it. In an article entitled "Doubting Calvinists," Patton mentions how a fellow Calvinist acquaintance of his was even at the point of suicide due to this doctrine of election.[12] Why? Because he "felt that his Calvinistic theology prevented him from ever having such assurance."[13] What a terrible conundrum!

The Problem with the Arminian View

In the Arminian approach to the doctrine of hell, God is, for lack of a better word, nicer. Instead of electing some for heaven and some for hell, "free" human agents do so. God simply allows for them to make the choice to suffer for all eternity. And, while this seems sensible on the surface—that is, it certainly *feels* as if we have the freedom to make such choices—once we pull on the threads a bit, the whole thing begins to unravel.

To start: What are we actually talking about when we talk about freedom and the will? For most of us in today's modern Western world, it is a given that freedom is best thought of as "the absolute spontaneity of the will."[14] What most lay folks don't realize, however, is that this assumed understanding wasn't fully developed until somewhat recently, initially by a fourteenth-century Franciscan friar named William Ockham and then, roughly four centuries later, by German philosopher Immanuel Kant. Essentially, what they both state is that human freedom is contingent upon the autonomous self. Philosopher Ric Machuga explains it this way: "Autonomous freedom is an 'all-or-nothing' affair. By definition it requires complete independence of all physical cause. Whenever this condition is met, people are free because it doesn't matter if they choose good or evil."[15]

But, what if "freedom" isn't best thought of as the ability to *arbitrarily* choose chicken instead steak, or right over wrong even, but as having one's will positioned toward something deeper and more meaningful? The latter, affirms David Bentley Hart:

> On any cogent account, free will is a power inherently purposive, teleological, primordially oriented toward the good, and shaped by that transcendental appetite to the degree that a soul can recognize the good for what it is. No one can *freely* will the evil as

evil; one can take the evil for the good, but that does not alter the prior transcendental orientation that wakens all desire. To see the good truly is to desire it insatiably; not to desire it is not to have known it, and so never to have been free to choose it.[16]

For an illustration of what Hart is saying, Donald J. Williams, Professor of English Literature, draws an apt analogy:

> The essence of human freedom within the powers of the world… is illustrated in Frodo's struggle on Amon Hen. His will seems overpowered both by the call of the Eye of Sauron wanting to find him and a voice commanding him to take off the ring so that Sauron will fail to do so. "The two powers strove in him. For a moment, perfectly balanced between their piercing points, he writhed, tormented. Suddenly he was aware of himself again. Frodo, neither the Voice nor the Eye: free to choose and with one remaining instant in which to do so. He took the Ring off his finger."[17] We find the essence of our humanity, our identity as children of Iluvatar, in those moments when, neither voice nor eye, we show our freedom within the bounds of the world by choosing the right.[18]

When we fail to choose "the good" or "the right," instead opting for "the bad" or "the wrong," it always seems to presuppose a bondage of some kind. In Frodo's grappling on Amon Hen, had he indeed kept the Ring on, one would have to conclude he did so because his will was overpowered by Sauron's. What other reason would there be?

Likewise, and more relevant to our discussion on hell, should we as "free" moral agents make choices that lead us into a state of perpetual misery—the fires of hell or of Mt. Doom—one would have to conclude a will that is either in complete ignorance to the situation and/or in captivity to some power or principality lording over them. (Think of Gollum's enslavement to the Ring.) Karl Barth once put it like this: "Disobedience is not a choice, but the incapacity of the man who is no longer or not yet able to choose in real freedom."[19] And so, piggybacking on this line of thinking, philosopher Thomas Talbott concludes:

> No one rational enough to qualify as a free moral agent could possibly prefer an objective horror—the outer darkness, for example—to eternal bliss, nor could any such person both experience the horror of separation from God and continue to regard it as a desirable state. The Augustinian idea that the damned are subjected to punishment against their will at least makes coherent sense, but the Arminian idea that the damned freely choose horror over bliss, hell over heaven, makes no coherent sense at all.[20]

There are, of course, rebuttals to this. The cleverest comes from Arminian philosopher Jerry Walls in his book *Hell: The Logic of Damnation*. In essence, Walls agrees with Talbott that no truly free agent chooses damnation over salvation, hell over heaven, but instead that the damned make initially free choices that trap them in a state of willful ignorance or bondage, thus leading them down the road to perdition.[21] In other words, it's not that people are simply making one final, free choice about their ultimate fate, but rather, that they are making a long series of choices that, while once upon a time free, have since become corrupted and enslaving.

This rationale, however, suffers from a fatal flaw. Allow me to explain.

When we make choices, it is always in our best interest to have the necessary information in order to make the good choice. In fact, if we are talking about our eternal fate, it is of utmost importance. So, should an initial choice be made that sends us down the road to bondage to sin, and subsequently, to hell, that initial choice can hardly be said to be made "freely," that is, free of any ignorance as to what such a choice would actually entail. It is always presupposed by some ignorance or bondage for without such ignorance or bondage, such a choice would never be made in the first place. As Eric Reitan notices: "Either the choice to be in one of these states is always based on a previous choice to be in one of these states, ad infinitum, such that we never arrive at a choice that is truly free; or there is some initial ignorance or bondage to desire that is not chosen based on any similar state, and hence could not be the result of a free choice."[22]

To see how this may work in the real world, consider the following example:

> A young boy is raised in a family sympathetic to ISIS. While yet in his diapers, he is taught that Jews are evil. And not only them, but all those who oppose (their understanding of) Islam—including other Muslims! Day after day, week after week, month after month, year after year, this viscous indoctrination

is crammed into his impressionable mind. The justification, he is told, is that the Qur'an is the Word of Allah, and that it is clearly written that his will is for the enemies of Islam to convert or perish. And should any of his family—including the young boy—ever reject this, they too should die.

Are we surprised, then, that when this boy (or so very many others like him) becomes a man, he'll likely join ISIS or some other terrorist organization and aspire to blow up others in the name of Allah? We shouldn't be!

So, it seems quite reasonable, then, to think that humans in situations like these never possess the type of "freedom" necessary to make an informed decision about God, humanity, or what salvation truly means. For example, do we not fail in finding a time or place where we could look back upon this boy's life and say "that is the initial free choice he made that led him down the road to willful ignorance and bondage?" Hence, could we really say that this young boy ever possessed the type of initial free choice Walls argues is necessary for one to choose damnation? The answer seems clear: *no*. Moreover, given the ridiculously broad range of personal situations the lot of humanity has fallen into over the eons—i.e., the ghastly suffering endured by an overwhelming number of souls—as well as the sheer ignorance and incompetence our mind and will so often fall prey to, the whole free will argument for the doctrine of hell, as Hart concludes, "becomes quite insufferable" even.[23]

AN ANTHROPOLOGICAL CONSIDERATION

This argument only becomes exceedingly more insufferable when it is confronted with the modern anthropological insights of René Girard.

If you recall, in chapter 3 we explored how human desires are predominantly mimetic, or in other words, imitative. Simply put, after our basic needs are met, without having one another to take on as *models*, we wouldn't really know what to desire. As Girard writes:

> If our desires were not mimetic, they would be forever fixed on predetermined objects; they would be a particular form of instinct. Human beings could no more change their desire than cows their appetite for grass. Without mimetic desire there would be neither freedom nor humanity.[24]

What this means is that freedom can never be found within the autonomous self because the autonomous self doesn't exist. That is why we are interdividuals, not individuals.[25] We are tied up, mimetically, with those around us and should the "ego self" actually be isolated and contained within what we call "I"—as we moderns say it is—it would be reduced to rubble, a shadow of what it once was. It would be enslaved to isolation, solitary confinement of the worst kind. (Just think of what happens to a prison inmate when they are consigned to "the hole" for any length of time.)

Yet, an issue remains. Perhaps we can even say it is a paradox: If what makes us human is not only bound up in taking on others as mimetic models, but also leads to the powers and principalities that *enslave* our world—*which it most certainly does*—how can we ever call ourselves "free?" And further, how should we then think about what it means to be saved from this?

All Set Free

JESUS' VIEW OF FREE WILL

The passage that best captures how Jesus seemed to think about freedom of the will comes from John 8:31–35:

> Then Jesus said to the Jews who had believed in him, "If you continue in my word, you are truly my disciples; and you will know the truth, and the truth will *make you free*...Very truly, I tell you, everyone who commits sin is a slave to sin...So if the Son *makes you free*, you will be free indeed." (emphasis mine)

Contrary to the modern notion of the autonomous human, where freedom is found in the complete and utter spontaneity of what we call "the self," here Jesus talks about a will that is *made* free. That is to say, our will and its relation to freedom is not fixed; it is, first and foremost, enslaved to the systems our religions and cultures place it under (i.e., the principalities and powers, the Law, the flesh, and so on). But then, through Christ Jesus, it is delivered from such a state.

This doesn't mean Jesus sets people free *against* their will. May it never be! Remember, our will is, as Hart puts it, "purposive, teleologically, [and] primordially oriented toward the good."[26] In other words, while it indeed finds itself so often enslaved, it is a will that also finds its roots in the very goodness of God, a will that has a purpose, an end goal if you will. After all, we are all made in the image and likeness of God. As the writer of John's prologue says, "In the beginning was the Logos, and the Logos was with God, and the Logos was God...and was the light of some people" (John 1:1, 4). Oh, wait, that's not how it goes: The Logos is the light of all Christians. Shit, that's still not right: The Logos is the light of *all people*. That is simply to say, all people bear with them the spark of the divine. This part of us always says yes to God; it's the ego, rooted in all the societal and religious programming we undergo, that needs freeing. And that deliverance is always for our own good!

So, in setting all of our wills free, in bringing all flesh to salvation (Luke 3:6)—indeed, in drawing *all* people toward himself (John 12:32)—Jesus takes all of us *toward* freedom and *away from* all that holds us in bondage and captivity: sin (John 8:34; Rom 6:18), iniquity (Acts 8:23), the powers and principalities (Rom 8:37–39), death and our fear and anxiety over it (Rom 5:14, 17; Heb 2:14–15), our dying bodies (Rom 7:24), the devil (1 Tim 3:7; 2 Tim 2:26), and all other forms slavery takes. These are the dark powers that cannot comprehend the type of deliverance the light of Christ brings (John 1:5). So, to that end, as Jesus himself said: "The slave does not have a permanent place in the household; the son has a place there forever" (John 8:35).

PAUL'S CORPORATE SOTERIOLOGY

It is reasonable to think that Paul had a similar understanding of the will in mind. For him—like Jesus—the will wasn't about having the freedom to arbitrarily make choices, but was, in fact, something so enslaved that only the deliverance of God could overcome it. This is seen most obviously when he admits: "For I do not do the good I want, but the evil I do not want is what I do" (Rom 7:19). And again: "For God has *imprisoned all* in disobedience so that he may be merciful to all" (Rom 11:32, emphasis mine). And yet again, from the book of Acts: "Let it be known to you therefore, my brothers, that through this man [Jesus] forgiveness of sins is proclaimed to you; by this Jesus everyone who believes is *set free* from all those sins from which you could not be freed by the law of Moses" (Acts 13:38–39, emphasis mine).

To that end, for Paul, the deliverance of God he himself experienced on the Damascus Road *never* gets reduced to being about one person or even one group of people, as so many Augustinians would have us believe. Rather, when it comes to this God-initiated salvation—this "setting free" as it were—things are always put in corporate terms and void of dividing lines so that none may boast (Eph 2:9). In other words, salvation isn't so much about individually being set free—as if we are individuals and not interdividuals—but about us all being *graciously* set free together; predestined to be one body united in Christ. Anything less, or so it certainly seems, grants one the ability to boast in something—one's own faith, for instance—other than Christ.

Now, some would be inclined to disagree. In fact, given the unpopularity of the Universalist position these days, I'm guessing *most* would disagree. And this is perfectly fine. But, to do so would be to miss the obvious universality of Paul's salvific message, which is driven home in three distinct passages.[28] First, in Romans 5:12-19 (all emphasis mine):

> Therefore, just as sin came into the world through one man, and death came through sin, and so death spread to *all* because *all* have sinned—sin was indeed in the world before the law, but sin is not reckoned when there is no law. Yet death exercised dominion from Adam to Moses, even over those whose sins were not like the transgression of Adam, who is a type of the one who was to come.
>
> But the free gift is not like the trespass. For if the *many* died through one man's trespass, much more surely have the grace of

God and the free gift in the grace of the one man, Jesus Christ, abounded for the *many*. And the free gift is not like the effect of one man's sin. For the judgment following one trespass brought condemnation, but the free gift following many trespasses brings justification. If, because of the one man's trespass, death exercised dominion through that one, much more surely will those who receive the abundance of grace and the free gift of righteousness exercise dominion in life through the one man, Jesus Christ.

Therefore just as one man's trespass led to condemnation for *all*, so one man's act of righteousness leads to justification and life for *all*. For just as by one man's disobedience the *many* were made sinners, so by the one man's obedience the *many* will be made righteous.

And again, in 1 Corinthians 15:22–28 (all emphasis mine):

For as *all* die in Adam, so *all* will be made alive in Christ. But each in his own order: Christ the first fruits, then at his coming those who belong to Christ. Then comes the end, when he hands over the kingdom to God the Father, after he has destroyed every ruler and every authority and power. For he must reign until he has put *all* enemies under his feet. The last enemy to be destroyed is death. For "God has put *all* things in subjection under his feet." But when it says, "*All* things are put in subjection," it is plain that this does not include the one who put *all* things in subjection under him. When *all* things are subjected to him, then the Son himself will also be subjected to the one who put *all* things in subjection under him, so that God may be *all* in *all*.

Finally, in Colossians 1:15–20 (all emphasis mine):[29]

He is the image of the invisible God, the firstborn of all creation; for in him *all* things in heaven and on earth were created, things visible and invisible, whether thrones or dominions or rulers or powers—*all* things have been created through him and for him. He himself is before *all* things, and in him *all* things hold together. He is the head of the body, the church; he is the beginning, the firstborn from the dead, so that he might come to have first place in *everything*. For in him *all* the fullness of God was pleased to dwell, and through him God was pleased to reconcile to himself *all* things, whether on earth or in heaven, by making peace through the blood of the cross.

Suffice it to say, for Paul, being set free (i.e., "saved") is always initiated and actualized by God. That is the point of his insistence that "no one can say 'Jesus is Lord' except by the Holy Spirit" (1 Cor 12:3). In other words, it is the Holy Spirit that compels us to reconcile to God through Christ. We are but conduits for this grace. Sure, to know that is to trust it, but not knowing it doesn't change what *has* been done and what *will* be done—that "in Christ God was reconciling the world to himself, not counting their trespasses against them" (2 Cor 5:19), that on the cross Jesus was drawing all people to himself (John 12:32), that by one man's act of righteousness all will be made righteous (Rom 5:19), that one day "all will be made alive in Christ" (1 Cor 15:22), and that, in the fullness of time, "every knee should bend, in heaven and on earth and under the earth, and every tongue should give praise that Jesus Christ is Lord, to the glory of the Father" (Phil 2:9–11). This is our blessed hope, our promise—even our *destiny* if you'd like—that

> This is our blessed hope, our promise— even our *destiny* if you'd like—that through Jesus' life, death, and resurrection, all of us will be *dragged* to him so that God may be "all in all."

through Jesus' life, death, and resurrection, all of us will be *dragged* to him so that God may be "all in all." Finally, then, we'll all be free; we'll be home, forever in the kingdom of God.

9
The Wrath (of God): Revealed from Heaven or from the Human Heart?

"I consider it a gentle understatement to say, 'The final wrath of God will be terrible—indescribable pain.' And putting the first and second truths together: This terrible, indescribable painful wrath will last forever. There will be no escape."[1]

—JOHN PIPER

"Biblically, it [wrath] is the divine judgment upon sin and sinners. It does not merely mean that it is a casual response by God to ungodliness, but carries the meaning of hatred, revulsion, and indignation."[2]

—CARM THEOLOGICAL DICTIONARY

As the writer to the Hebrews acknowledges, it is indeed a terrible thing to suffer the wrath of God (Heb 10:31). But what does that even mean? For many, it is plain: God is going to strike some of us down (in this life and/or the next) and then have us either metaphorically or literally burned alive for all eternity should we fail in getting things right (i.e., repenting and turning to Jesus).

One problem (among many) with this view is that it caricaturizes God as an angry deity, a la Zeus of Greek mythological fame. Just do a Google image search of Zeus and you will see what I mean: there he stands, like a total asshole, pointing the accusatory finger, a lightning bolt primed and ready to strike at-will. Honestly, what is the tangible difference between Zeus and how famed Calvinist Jonathan Edwards describes the Christian God?

> The God that holds you over the pit of hell, much as one holds a spider or some loathsome insect over the fire, abhors you, and is dreadfully provoked. His wrath towards you burns like fire; he looks upon you as worthy of nothing else but to be cast into the fire. He is of purer eyes than to bear you in his sight, you are ten thousand times as abominable in his eyes as the most hateful, venomous serpent is in ours.[3]

Despite such caricatures, I *will*, nevertheless, readily admit that the wrath of God is a very real concept, one that should not be taken lightly. However, if we are going to take the Bible seriously, wrath, in my estimations, needs to be nuanced because, as the writer of 1 John puts it: "God is love" *and* "God is light and in him there is no darkness at all" (1 John 1:5; 4:8). To that end, the wrath of God must be thought of within the context that God's very nature *is* love, and not the other way around.

Furthermore, given that Christians profess Jesus Christ as the "fullness of God in bodily form," it seems beyond reasonable to say that theology begins, not in gloriously lofty adjectives, but on a hill called Golgotha. A hill, mind you, where a God-Man died preaching enemy love and forgiveness (Luke 23:34). Pardon the pun, but Luther hammered this home in theses nineteen through twenty-one of *The Heidelberg Disputation* of 1518. What he made clear is that theology mustn't begin with glory—God-concepts raised to the nth degree—but with the suffering Christ whom we pierced.

Again, as Christians, we should get this. Yet, more often than not, we don't.

How Did We Get Here?

So, how have we gotten to a place where the love of God as revealed through Christ is forced to take a backseat to such concepts as God's "wrath?" My hunch is that the answer can be found in how folks are reading their bibles.

Let me explain.

As we discussed in chapter 3, the biblical journey is not a simple one. We don't get from point A to point B in a nice, straight line. There are twists and turns and often, two steps forward are followed by one step back. Due to this, the concept of "God's wrath" ebbs and flows alongside other theological doctrines.

Early on in the journey, there is very little nuance. Think, for a moment, of the tale of Sodom and Gomorrah. Within the walls of these two cities, corruption and wickedness is pervasive; so much so that not even ten righteous inhabitants could be found (Gen 18:32). Things are so disgustingly vile that when two angels visit a man named Lot, they are quickly surrounded by "all the people to the last man" who had hopes that an epic gangrape could ensue (Gen 19:4–5). To quell the attack, Lot offers his virgin daughters instead (I told you this place was vile!) This tactic doesn't work, however, and so the men lustfully pursue. But, through some *deus-ex-machina-style* intervention, the rapists are struck blind. Eventually, Lot and a few family members escape.

After the family flees to safety, the wrath of God pours out: sulfur and fire rain down on both cities and they are laid to waste. Every inhabitant, every plant that grows on the ground… utterly destroyed. For good measure, Lot's wife is even turned into a pillar of salt for looking back on the ruin (Gen 19:26).

Let's go on.

Turn your attention to Lamentations 2. Here, the prophet Jeremiah despairs over the Israelites' destruction at the hands of the Babylonians. What is so incredibly striking is that while human beings are literally responsible for the annihilation of Jerusalem—that is to say, Babylon destroyed Jerusalem—according to Jeremiah, it is first and foremost God's doing. Just desserts for their wicked ways! He is pretty clear about this:

- The Lord is angry (v. 1)
- The Lord destroys without mercy (v. 2)
- The Lord cuts down (v. 3)
- The Lord kills (v. 4)
- The Lord lays waste (v. 5)
- The Lord is fierce with indignation (v. 6)
- The Lord disowns (v. 7)
- The Lord's hand destroys (v. 8)
- The Lord causes ruin (v. 9)

This causes the ghastliest sort of human suffering imaginable:
- Infants and babies faint in the street (v. 11)
- Children die on their mothers' bosom (v. 12)
- Rest and respite are not to be found (v. 18)
- Children go hungry (v. 19)
- Women eat their children (v. 20; 4:10)

Holy crap, Batman!

At first glance, these passages indeed give the impression that God is, for lack of a better description, a wrathful monster. But, what if (already acknowledging the bumpy road the Bible takes us on), we get a later view of "the wrath of God" that isn't so archaic and emesis-inducing? What if these literalized depictions of wrath and vengeance are "reworked" so as to not do violence to our theology of the cross?

Well, that is just what the Apostle Paul does in two very distinct places. But, before we get to his writings, I thought it best to mention his firsthand encounter with the risen Christ. This way, we can bear in mind Paul's real-world experiences—including one that converted him from violent zealot to nonviolent apostle—that would heavily inform his later theology, including what we call "the wrath of God."

Paul's Nuancing of God's Wrath

THE ROAD TO DAMASCUS

In Acts 26, Paul tells his story. He admits, regretfully, that prior to his "conversion," he not only locked up followers of Jesus, but advocated for their death as well. Everything changes, however, while on his way to Damascus. Still breathing murderous threats (Acts 9:1–2), he is hit with a flash of brilliant light that knocks him right on his ass (Acts 26:13–14).

"Oh no!" Paul must have thought. "I'm a dead man."

The risen Jesus questions him: "Saul, Saul, why are you persecuting me?"

This must have been a death-blow to Paul. The very "Christians" he was inflicting violence against were following the nonviolent one whom God raised from the dead. And more than that, the very issue Paul is confronted with is the violence he believed God desired.

> The issue here isn't whether a person is a Jew or a Christian or a Muslim or a Hindu. The issue is redemptive violence.

But then, Paul *isn't* met with violence. No! He is met with the gracious wrath of Christ—if we can even call it that—who warns: "It hurts *you* to kick against the goads" (Acts 26:14, emphasis mine). In other words, what Paul, in all his wrath, was doing not only hurt his victims, but hurt him as well. Essentially, his behavior was as beneficial as slamming one's head up against a brick wall.

So, with regard to our discussion, three things are important for us to glean from this story.

1. The issue here isn't whether a person is a Jew or a Christian or a Muslim or a Hindu. The issue is redemptive violence. The issue is zeal. The issue is believing the wrath of God is "such and such," that

we act it out violently against the other. We can call this projection, and any divine wrath that involves violence is just that.

2. The wrath Saul was engaging in is met by the "wrath" of Christ, which is to say, the love and mercy and compassion of Christ. It is "wrath" in that it is in your face and cuts to the chase. But, it subverts Saul's human notion of wrath by confronting his violence peacefully.

3. Jesus gives a warning about where human wrath leads. To kick against the goads is to engage in a fruitless endeavor. Violence and zeal and persecution and "us vs. them" thinking all fall into this category. This is what Paul had to understand prior to becoming a servant of the peaceful gospel of Christ (Rom 1:1; Eph 6:15).

ROMANS 1

Now, with Paul's conversion experience in mind, let's get to our initial passage. First though, since we are diving back into Romans, a brief recap of the gist of Douglas Campbell's rhetorical reading of the book:

> Within the first four chapters of the letter, Paul lays out a theological debate between himself and some false teachers who have besmirched his name and taught a false gospel. Included in this supposed "gospel" is not only an infusion of the Law—Sabbath-keeping, kosher meals, and the male circumcision ritual—but an eschatology full of divine wrath against all who are unrighteous (generally the Gentiles; see

Wisdom of Solomon 13–14). One of Paul's major goals in writing a letter this way is to expose the false teachers' "gospel" as *self*-condemning (Rom 2:1). In other words, Paul wants to use the logic of the teachers in order to put on display the futility of their view (Rom 2:1–4:3).

What is fascinating, then, is how Paul, in subverting the argument of the false teachers, draws on his experiential knowledge to also subvert the "common" Jewish-Christian understanding of God's wrath.

Here's how he does this.

When Paul introduces the "false gospel" in 1:18, he indeed begins by including the phrase *orge Theou*, or "wrath of God." Unfortunately, this is where most Western Christians seem to stop reading. But, if we read on to 1:24, 26, 28, we'll notice that this wrath gets rather nuanced when compared to how it is understood by many a Christian thinker:

- Verse 24: God *gave them up* in their lusts…

- Verse 26: God *gave them up* to degrading passions…

- Verse 28: God *gave them up* to a debased mind…

Simply put, the wrath of God in 1:18 is really God giving people over to the natural consequences of living a life oriented toward wickedness. One could call it *reaping what you sow*.

But, Paul doesn't stop there. Once he gets into the meat of the "debate," while speaking in his own "voice," he nuances things further by never again using the phrase *orge Theou*. Rather, he opts to simply call it "the wrath."[4] Why? He tells us: "By *your* hard and impenitent heart *you* are storing up wrath for *yourself*" (Rom 2:5, emphasis mine). In other words, it is humanity who brings down wrath upon her own head by acting in a certain way, that is, in an un-Christlike way. And, when we do, we engage in an exercise of futility, a "kicking against the goads."

So, contrary to the writer of Genesis 19 and the prophet Jeremiah, according to Paul the wrath of God should not be viewed as some cosmic violence that rains down from the heavens, but as God allowing us to reap the fruit of our self-destructive ways. My friend and scholar, Brad Jersak, makes this point:

> What Paul actually says is that God through Christ was saving us from the wrath. Period. We are not to believe that Jesus is saving us from God the Father, but from the consequences intrinsic to sin itself, namely death…So yes, God rescues us from "the wrath," from sin, from death. Wrath then, is not the punishment of God but our experience of the intrinsic and fatal consequences of sin—of rejecting God's mercy.[5]

Think of the prodigal son story. When the youngest son demands his inheritance, only to squander it all, the father cannot be said to be directly responsible even though he gave his son the money. The son is responsible. Sure, the father allows the son to reap the natural consequences of acting in the way he did, but it's the son's behavior that "stores up wrath for himself."

> According to Paul the wrath of God should not be viewed as some cosmic violence that rains down from the heavens, but as God allowing us to reap the fruit of our self-destructive ways.

Likewise, think of what happened in 70 CE. When Jesus' people refuse to listen to his admonitions and they are slaughtered en masse, the Father cannot be said to be directly responsible even though he "allows" it to happen. The people are responsible. Rome is responsible (centuries before that it was the Babylonians). Utter destruction is what happens just about every damn time we "store up wrath for ourselves."

Yet, in spite of this, Paul and other New Testament writers teach that God never gives up on us. (Can we imagine a time when the father would refuse to run and greet the infamous prodigal?) While we are, for a time indeed given over to our wickedness (Rom 1:24, 26, 28), we are also sent deliverance "while we were yet sinners" (Rom 5:8). Not in hopes that we can be spared from God himself—as if Jesus ever talked about such an absurd thing—but so all of us can be saved from the wages of our sin (Rom 6:23). That is to say, we can be saved from death and the destructive wrath our fear of death brings (see chapters 1 and 7).

> Can we imagine a time when the father would refuse to run and greet the infamous prodigal?

1 CORINTHIANS 10

If you recall, in chapter 3 we explored the story from Numbers 25. Do you remember how the plague that ends up wiping out 24,000 Israelites is brought about by the "fierce anger of the Lord" that kindled against Israel for getting down and dirty with the Moabites? Well, in 1 Corinthians 10, Paul is going to comment on this story, but he's going to put a creative spin on it. Notice:

- Verse 9: "We must not put the Lord to the test, as some of them did, and were *destroyed by serpents*."

- Verse 10: "And do not complain as some of them did, and were *destroyed by the destroyer*."

Now, we won't yet comment on who (or what) the serpent or the destroyer is (we'll save that for Appendix B). Simply notice that Paul is reworking where the wrath that befell the Israelites can be traced. Sure, the people tested God; they were disobedient, and experienced destruction (24,000 deaths; cf. Num 25:9). But, whereas the Old Testament writer gives God the credit for the dubiously high body count, Paul reworks things and attributes the carnage to "the destroyer."

I want to note that this is not, however, merely a Pauline way of exegeting the Israelites' history. The same sort of interpretive move away from *God-as-wrathful-destroyer* can be seen in the Hebrew Scriptures themselves. In two separate accounts of the same story, notice who each writer deems responsible for inciting King David to take a census of Israel (one that kills 70,000 people; cf. 2 Sam 25:15):

- 2 Samuel 24:1: "Again the anger of *the Lord* was kindled against Israel, and he incited David against them, saying, 'Go, count the people of Israel and Judah.'"

- 1 Chronicles 21:1: "*Satan* stood up against Israel, and incited David to count the people of Israel."

What is going on here is not what Evangelicals suggest—that God and Satan are working in cahoots, as if Satan is God's consigliere—but rather, that over the course of their journey, the Hebrew people moved from one theological place to another. The chronicler could no longer see the evil that happened because of this census—the death of 70,000 people—as something God ordained. Rather, it had to be placed upon the shoulders of

Satan, just as Paul placed the death of 24,000 Israelites squarely on the shoulders of "the destroyer."

In Closing

Indeed, it is a terrible thing to suffer the wrath of God. Paul experienced this directly, and after it knocked him on his back side, it forced him to reconsider everything he once believed. This can be a difficult thing to endure. But, as the writer of Hebrews puts it, "Now, discipline always seems painful rather than pleasant at the time, but later it yields the peaceful fruit of righteousness to those who have been trained by it" (Heb 12:11).

This is where the wrath of God differs from the wrath of Man. The wrath of God is a gracious wrath, driven by God's passionate love for humanity. The wrath of Man is a vengeful wrath, driven by our desire for sacrifice. Too often, we conflate the two and call our wrath "sacred." But, it is hardly that, for sacred wrath is non-sacrificial. In fact, it is "wrath" that invades worlds of sacrificial violence, tears down these strongholds, and replaces vengeance with agape love.

10
Kickin' Ass and Takin' Names

"In Revelation, Jesus is a Pride fighter with a tattoo down his leg, a sword in his hand and the commitment to make someone bleed. That is a guy I can worship. I cannot worship the hippie, diaper, halo Christ because I cannot worship a guy I can beat up." [1]

—MARK DRISCOLL

"Then the kings of the earth and the magnates and the generals and the rich and the powerful, and everyone, slave and free, hid in the caves and among the rocks of the mountain, calling to the mountains and rocks, 'Fall on us and hide us from the face of the one seated on the throne and from the wrath of the Lamb; for the great day of their wrath has come, and who is able to stand?"

—REVELATION 6:15-17

"Jesus is coming back," or so says the great majority of Christians. But when, and in what fashion, the Church has historically been at odds over. At the present, many take a stance like Driscoll's, where Jesus is coming back to kick ass and take—or rather, leave off—names.[2] Mike Bickle, director of the International House of Prayer, is one of these, and chillingly envisions the following future scenario:

> Jesus is actually on the earth marching up to Jerusalem from Egypt, and then from the south through Jordan. He is killing his enemies…he actually kills millions of people. The time it takes to actually kill them takes time. He marches up through the land. It is a thirty-day process where he marches up from Egypt.[3]

For all intents and purposes, this is precisely the imaginative eschatological worldview that was handed to me when I was a child. The Rapture of the Church—a mere 200-year-old doctrine that states believers, the living *and* resurrected dead, will one-day skyrocket into the air to be caught up with Christ in the clouds[4]—was, of course, included. But, was I going to be among these? I never knew! Nevertheless, this apocalyptic worldview was starkly terrifying (to put it mildly). Instead of living the life a child should, it drove me to constantly daydream about "wars and rumors of wars (Mark 13:7)," so that I could always be on guard, always either ready for my jettisoning out of here, or to face the impending chaos should I be "left behind."

After a time, I grew weary of such a view. It was all too much to bear, and frankly, felt so disconnected from what I read in the gospels. There, Jesus' yoke was easy, and his burden light (Matt 11:30). But the second time around was going to be no such thing. Cross him, and you were going to be, like the Israelite and Midianite couple caught having sex in Numbers 25, "impaled in the sun," left as carrion for the birds and beasts of the field to gnaw on (Rev 19:17–19).

"How could such a split view of Jesus ever be reconciled?" I pondered.

To put it plainly, it can't, which brings me to my first major point: any future "apocalypse" of Christ Jesus *must be* consistent with the first "apocalypse" as testified to in the four gospels and then by the Apostle Paul. There are no two ways about it.

Let me explain why.

In Greek, the word "apocalypse" literally means "an unveiling." Most appropriately, with regards to Christian theology, it refers to an unveiling of the revelation of Christ Jesus, the *Logos* (Word) of God. The apocalypse of God in the first century was, most specifically, that his nature is "love" and "light" (1 John 1:5, 4:8) and that his Gospel is peace (Eph 6:5). How do we know? As Paul puts it, "in him [Christ] the whole fullness of deity dwells bodily (Col 2:9)." Or, to say it another way, God's nature was, is, and will always be like that of Christ Jesus (Heb 13:8) and that thinking about theology begins, not in glory, but at the foot of his cross. To that end, any notion of a split apocalypse—where on the one hand the nonviolent Logos of God was revealed in Jesus Christ (John 1:1–5) and on the other that he, sometime in the future, will be revealed as a bad-ass Pride fighter—is theologically absurd and should come to have no bearing on the peace-laden Gospel (Eph 6:5) of the One whom we build our foundation on (1 Cor 3:11).

> Any future "apocalypse" of Christ Jesus *must be* consistent with the first "apocalypse" as testified to in the four gospels and then by the Apostle Paul. There are no two ways about it.

Nevertheless, when we *do* assume a dualistic eschatology such as the one Driscoll and Bickle assume—one where the Universe is split, some to the blissful afterlife in the clouds and others, some of which are apparently actually whacked by Jesus himself, to the perpetual barbecue down below—we have a tendency to miss the overwhelming New Testament teaching that we "believers" are not only to anticipate, but help bring about, insofar as we are able, God's *wholly* restored kingdom "on earth as it is in heaven" (Matt 6:10). In other words, our Christian focus isn't to be so much on where our eternal destiny lay, although that certainly bears consideration, but on transforming the present reality *in light of* the post-resurrection eschatological truth that *all* death and *all* tears of sorrow will be done away with forever (Rev 21:4). N.T. Wright notices the very same focus among the early Christians:

> For the early Christians, the resurrection of Jesus launched God's new creation upon the world, beginning to fulfill the prayer Jesus taught his followers, that God's kingdom would come "on earth as it is in heaven" (Matt 6:10), and anticipating the "new heavens and a new earth" (Isa 65:17; 66:22; 2

Pet 3:13; Rev 21:1) promised by Isaiah and again in the New Testament…The early Christians were not very interested, in the way our world has been interested, in what happens to people immediately after they die. They were extremely interested in a topic many Western Christians in the last few hundred years have forgotten about altogether, namely the final new creation, new heavens and new earth joined together, and the resurrection of the body that will create new human beings to live in that new world.[5]

This is a view that, while in some ways uniquely Christian, draws many parallels with its Jewish parents. In the next section, we will explore how this prophetic trajectory, beginning with the Hebrew Scriptures and then culminating in the Christian apocalyptic book of Revelation, consistently portrays a hopeful vision of the end, not merely one that ends in death and destruction.

A Prophetic Vision of the End

THE JEWISH PROPHETS

Isaiah

Included in many of Isaiah's writings are visions of a glorious future; of a "New Jerusalem" shrouded in peace, one where even "the wolf and lamb shall feed together, [and] the lion shall eat straw like the ox" (Isa 11:5–7; 65:25). This is not simply to say that all of God's creatures will one day adopt a vegan lifestyle—although I suppose it's possible—but rather, that in a future time, or age, "all the nations," having beaten "their swords into plowshares, and their spears into pruning hooks," will live in peace in the City of God (Isa 2:2–4). In spite of all the conflict and trouble "the nations" cause Israel—and vice-versa I imagine—one day there will be perfect, divine tranquility. In spite of the "wicked" nations being rebellious and suffering defeat (Isa 34:1–2; 60:12, 20), they will one day bask in the light (Isa 60:3) of God's "new creation" (Isa 65:17; 66:22), bringing their "wealth" into the heavenly places (Isa 60:5, 11), honoring God's people all the while (Isa 60:14, 16).[6]

Jeremiah

Jeremiah envisions something similar. Like Isaiah, he too foresees a time where former enemy nations are restored by God. In chapter 48, the prophet tells of the destruction of Moab. These were, as Jeremiah says, a prideful people (Jer 48:29) who had a knack for boasting in false deeds (Jer 48:30); so much so that it leads to their ruin. Her people cry out over their fate (Jer 48:4) as they are "laid to waste" (Jer 48:20). Yet, after all this fiery judgement, God promises to "restore the fortunes of Moab in the latter days" (Jer 48:47). And again, in chapter 49, Jeremiah tells of a similar fate for Elam. After they have disaster and the sword of the Lord brought down upon them (Jer 49:37), killing their kings and officials (Jer 49:38), their fortunes are restored, again "in the latter days" (Jer 49:39).

Ezekiel

In Ezekiel, the infamous Sodomites experience a similar fate. Now, we all know the first part of Sodom's story, the part where she, alongside her sister city Gomorrah, are annihilated by fire and sulfur from heaven (Gen 19:24) for their depravity (Gen 19:1–11; Ezek 16:49–50). Ezekiel describes their wickedness as follows: "She and her daughters had pride, excess of food, and prosperous ease, but did not aid the poor and needy. They were haughty, and did abominable things before me." Some of those abominable things included, but were not limited to, a potential gang rape of a couple of angels (Gen 19:4–5). And so, they are nuked from above, and no one who stays in the city makes it out alive. In fact, even Lot's wife gets smote for daring to look back on the ruin (Gen 19:26). Yet, what is then quite striking is that in spite of this utter destruction, the prophet still anticipates a hopeful fate: "I will restore their fortunes, the fortunes of Sodom and her daughters (Ezek 16:53)."

Zechariah

The prophet Zechariah also anticipates a time of perpetual peace, one ushered in by the apocalypse of a future king—and not peace through force and enemy-slaying, but peace that overcomes such things:

> Rejoice greatly, O daughter Zion!
>   Shout aloud, O daughter Jerusalem!
> Lo, your king comes to you;
>   Triumphant and victorious is he,
> Humble and riding on a donkey,
>   On a colt, the foal of a donkey.
> He will cut off the chariot from Ephraim
>   And the war-horse from Jerusalem;
> And the battle bow shall be cut off,
>   And he shall command peace to the nations;
> His dominion shall be from sea to sea,
>   And from the River to the ends of the earth.
>   —Zech 9:9–10

In a completely subversive way, the king who comes to "command peace to the nations" rides in on a humble donkey instead of a proud war-horse. In fact, his triumph and victory is when he *cuts off* the horses and chariots of war, and when he *breaks* the bows of battle, not when he wields them fiercer than any other. In doing so, he is given dominion over *all the earth*, from sea to shining sea. That is to say, he is given dominion over all humanity; indeed, all the nations (Isa 52:15).

THE BOOK OF REVELATION

At first glance, one may assume the book of Revelation reads quite dissimilarly than that of the prophets. Indeed, we can all probably see why most of the violent images of Jesus coming back to send the great majority of humanity to hell arise from this book. The language here, at times, is brutal, the imagery stark. And not only that, but all of the horror that is said to be coming is attributed to "the Lamb," or in other words, Christ Jesus himself (Rev 6:16). A scary picture of God indeed!

However, as serious as we should take the warnings contained in this piece of literature, we shouldn't be too fixated on drawing our theological conclusions from it.

Let me explain.

As we explored earlier, the apocalypse of God is most wholly seen in the figure of the first-century Jesus of Nazareth, the figure whom God worked through to "reconcile all things" by freely offering forgiveness from the cross (Col 1:15–20; Luke 23:34), and by speaking the word of peace and mercy after it (John 20:19–23, 26; Heb 12:24). So, it is not as if in some future age this will fail to be. Of course not! For, as the writer to the Hebrews put it: "Jesus Christ is the same yesterday and today and forever" (Heb 13:8). That is to say, our God is an eternal God (Gen 21:33, Ps 90:1–4).

Having this in the forefront of our minds—as our lens so to speak—is what it means to be under a "theology of the cross." We could also call it Christocentric (centered on Christ) and if we emphasize the non-retributive Christ as the *eschaton*, or ultimate end/goal, we could say it is Christotelic. John 12:31–33 captures this idea beautifully (all emphasis mine):

> "*Now* is the judgment of this world; *now* the ruler of this world will be driven out. And I, when I am lifted up from the earth, will draw *all people* to myself." He said this to indicate the kind of death he was to die.[7]

As we've mentioned, the kind of death being spoken of was an earth-shattering one. It was the revelation of a God JUST. LIKE. JESUS. That means no matter what, Christ's life, death, resurrection, and ascension determine how we think about *anything*, including the book of Revelation. Not the other way around!

That being said, in John's Revelation this "theology of the cross" theme *is* in fact introduced, as odd as that may initially sound. To begin, in Revelation 5, John envisions a scroll that, at the onset, is unable to be opened by anyone "in heaven or on earth or under the earth" (Rev 5:3). Because it is obviously an important scroll, and something that certainly must be opened, the fact that as of yet it hasn't been causes John great grief, to weep bitterly even (Rev 5:4). Quickly though, one of the elders comforts him: "Do not weep. See, the Lion of the tribe of Judah, the Root of David, has conquered, so that he can open the scroll and its seven seals" (Rev 5:5). Then, obviously expecting to see a lion, John turns and instead, sees a lamb as if slain (Rev 5:6). What a revelation this is! Sure, like lions are wont to do, Christ has conquered, but he has done so by *behaving* as a slain lamb. Similar to the Suffering Servant from Isaiah, then, all power and authority is subverted and given to one whom nobody expects (Isa 52:15), and it is he who is worthy to open the scroll.

> Like lions are wont to do, Christ has conquered, but he has done so by *behaving* as a slain lamb.

When we come to all the "wrath of the Lamb" talk in the following chapter, we must bear this in mind. Wrath, here, like in Paul's letter to the Romans, is a very specific and nuanced wrath (Rom 2:5). It is the giving over to the natural consequences of a humanity that refuses to care for the "least of these," for one example (Matt 25:31–46). Brad Jersak puts it like this:

> "The wrath of the Lamb" is a metaphor for God's consent ('giving over') to the intrinsic self-destructive consequences (natural and supernatural) of humankind's rebellion. It is wrath because we experience these consequences in ultraviolent ways—as if God were angry—but the Lamb is only indirectly complicit because, he operates by Lamb-like consent rather than coercive intervention.[8]

This "giving over" is seen, most strikingly, all throughout Revelation 6. And, as Jersak notes, the calamity that takes place after the Lamb opens the seals is purely anthropological. It is humanity and her persistence toward violence, for instance, that empowers the four riders: the white rider conquers with a *bow* (Rev 6:2—contra John 12:15; Zech 9:8–9), the red rider takes peace with a *sword* (Rev 6:4—contra Matt 26:51–52), the black rider's economic *scales* are imbalanced (Rev 6:6—contra Matt 25:31–46; Luke 4:18–19; 6:20, 24; 16:19–31), and the pale green rider, whose name was Death and Hades, kills with sword, famine, pestilence, and beasts of the earth (Rev 6:8—contra Isa 11:6; Matt 26:51–52; Mark 1:40–45; Luke 17:11–19; John 6:1–15). Then, after this doom befalls the world, the martyrs, like Abel long, long ago, cry out for vengeance (Gen 4:10; Rev 6:10—contra Heb 12:24).

Yet, none will come, for the blood of Jesus speaks a better word than Abel (Heb 12:24). Any vengeance that is coming, then, is only that which we have stored up for ourselves by our hard and impenitent hearts, as Paul once put it (Rom 2:5). Toward the end of Revelation 6, it is described, in classic Jewish fashion, in the most apocalyptic of ways: the sun goes dark, the moon becomes like blood, the stars fall to the earth, the sky vanishes like a rolled-up scroll, and mountains and islands are removed from their place (Rev 6:12–14; Isa 13; 34). *Kings* shutter and declare it the end of the world, for the "great day of their wrath" is upon them (Rev 6:17).

But is this truly describing the end of world? Yes and no, says Jersak:

> The apocalyptic language here is borrowed directly from Isaiah 13, 34 and Matthew 24. Isaiah 13 ascribes the cosmic meltdown to the Day of the Lord when God in his anger destroys the Babylonian empire. In similar language, Isaiah 34 refers

to the retributive vengeance that completely wipes out the nation of Edom. And in Matthew 24, Jesus cites these texts to announce the obliteration of Jerusalem within one generation. In every case, the cosmic imagery refers to temporal earthly events already fulfilled in history through the destruction of a city, kingdom or empire by military sieges from foreign armies.[9]

Some would be inclined to push back and say that the events described in Revelation, contrary to that of Isaiah and Matthew, are not at all about events already fulfilled in history but rather, events that are to come. And perhaps to some extent they would be correct. Perhaps not *all* of the events of Revelation have been fulfilled. That is fair. Then again, perhaps others are fulfilled over and over ad nauseam. Perhaps it is more than either/or, but rather, both/and. Perhaps the two opposing cosmic entities—New Jerusalem and Babylon—are such that the events that play out in the book are really a way to talk about the two paths humanity can choose to walk down. Perhaps this choice was directly applicable in the first century, in the centuries that followed, and even today and on into the future.

Perhaps.

Nevertheless, no matter how you slice it, two things we can trust. First, any "end of the world" event will always be brought about by wrath and vengeance that we *store up for ourselves*. The Lamb simply permits it, as he did in the first century, as he does throughout history, and as he will do until this age passes into the next. But, don't think that, in the end, the Lamb won't find a way to be victorious. May we never believe that! There always remains hope because no matter how brutal the cosmic battles may be, no matter how dire things become for any who oppose the Lamb (Rev 20:15), there is a promise that waits to be fulfilled, and the *whole* creation groans for this future time (Rom 8:18–25).

The Gates of New Jerusalem

Almost shockingly—given the stark imagery throughout the book—the conclusion to Revelation foretells of a *promising* and *hopeful* future that is not unlike the one Isaiah painted long before. In Isaiah 2, the prophet foresees a coming time when *all the nations* shall stream to the Lord's house (Isa 2:2–3). In Revelation 22, the invitation is sent out: "The Spirit and the bride say, 'Come.' And let everyone who hears say, 'Come.' And let everyone who is thirsty come. Let anyone who wishes take the water of life as a gift." (Rev 22:17) To whom is this invitation sent? Those outside the city, of course. But who is outside the city? Both Revelation 21:8 and 22:15 tell us:

- Rev 21:8: "As for the cowardly, the faithless, the polluted, the murderers, the fornicators, the sorcerers, the idolaters, and all liars, their place will be in the lake that burns with fire and sulfur."

- Rev 22:15: "Outside are the dogs and sorcerers and fornicators and murderers and idolaters, and everyone who loves and practices falsehood."

To put it simply, to be in the lake of fire is to be outside the gates of New Jerusalem. There are no two ways about it. It is a fate suffered by not only the wicked listed above, but also the kings of the earth and "the nations" who wage war against the Lamb (Rev 6:15; 17:14 19:18–19; 20:8). The bad guys, if you will.

So, the question is: Will they come? Will they take up the call? "Yes, one day" says John: "The nations will walk by its light, and the kings of the earth will bring their glory into it" (Rev

21:24). That is the hope anyway. And it's the same hope Isaiah had: "Nations shall come to your light, and kings to the brightness of your dawn" (Isa 60:3).

This isn't some cheap invitation, however. Nay! Those who enter the perpetually open gates of New Jerusalem (Isa 60:11; Rev 21:25) in order to drink from the life-giving waters (Isa 55:2; Rev 22:1–2) and partake of the tree that is for the "healing of the nations" (Rev 22:3) will have to have their "robes washed in the blood of the Lamb" (Rev 22:14). That is to say, those outside the city, once they hear the Spirit and the bride's call to "come," will have to draw near to Christ in order to experience the healing that is *perpetually* and *mercifully* set before them (see Ps 136, where God's "steadfast love" is declared twenty-six times).

Concluding Thoughts

Theologically, what can we conclude from this? Given the fact that the book of Revelation is based off a vision, probably not much. But, what cannot be emphasized enough is that the Lord Jesus Christ is the same yesterday, today, and forever (Heb 13:8). In other words, Christ's nature remains consistent, no matter the epoch, no matter the circumstance, no matter the situation. To that end, *if* Christ is coming back—and I continue to hold fast that Christ indeed is—it won't be to defeat his enemies with violence and war, but by destroying that which causes them to be an enemy in the first place, so that they can one day heed the call to "come" and be healed. Until that day, we can have hope. We can hope for a future time when everyone enters through the open gates to partake of the feast. We can share in Isaiah's hope, and Jeremiah's, and John the Revelator's. Dare I say, we can share in Jesus' hope, the savior of all people, especially of those who believe (1 Tim 4:10). And we can, as the bride of Christ, with tears in our eyes, continue to send out the invitation to "come" be reconciled to God!

> *If* Christ is coming back—and I continue to hold fast that Christ indeed is—it won't be to defeat his enemies with violence and war, but by destroying that which causes them to be an enemy in the first place, so that they can one day heed the call to "come" and be healed.

APPENDIX A
Many Voices, One Message

"They all were honored and glorified, not through themselves or their works or their righteous behavior, but through God's will. And we also, who have been called in Christ Jesus through his will, are not justified through ourselves or through our own wisdom or understanding or piety, or our actions done in holiness of heart, but through faith, for it is through faith that Almighty God has justified all men that have been from the beginning of time: to whom be glory for ever and ever. Amen."

—CLEMENT OF ROME, *FIRST EPISTLE TO THE CORINTHIANS*, XXXII

"The only-begotten Word, who is always present with the human race, united and mingled with his handiwork, according to the Father's pleasure, and incarnate, is himself Jesus Christ our Lord, who suffered for us, and rose again for us, and is to come again in the glory of the Father to raise up all flesh to manifest salvation, and to apply the rule of just judgement to all who were made by him. Thus there is one God the Father, as we have demonstrated, and one Christ Jesus our Lord who came in fulfillment of God's comprehensive design and consummates all things in himself. Man is in all respects the handiwork of God; thus he consummates man in himself: he was invisible and became visible; incomprehensible and made comprehensible; impassible and made passible; the Word, and made man; consummating all things in himself. That, as in things above the heavens and in the spiritual and invisible world the Word of God is supreme, so in the visible and physical realm he may have pre-eminence, taking to himself the primacy and appointing himself the head of the Church, that he may 'draw all things to himself' in due time."

—IRENAEUS, *ADVERSUS HAERESES*, III. XVI. 6

"The gospel says that 'many bodies of those who had fallen asleep arose'—clearly to a better state—the state of those who have been changed. There was then a kind of general movement and change as a result of the economy of the Savior. One righteous man does not differ from another in respect of his righteousness whether he be under the Law, or a Greek. For God is the Lord not of the Jews only but of all men, though he is more intimately the Father of those who know him…Those who lived good lives before the Law were reckoned as having faith, and were judged to be righteous. It is clear that those who were outside the Law because they spoke a different language, and yet had lived good lives, even if they were actually in Hades and 'in prison,' on hearing the voice of the Lord—either his own voice or that which operated through the Apostles—were converted and believed. For we remember that the Lord is 'the power of God'; and power could never be powerless.

Thus, I fancy, the goodness of God is proved, and the power of the Lord, to save with justice and equity displayed to those who turn to him, whether here or elsewhere. For the energizing power does not come only on men here; it is operative in all places and at all times."

—CLEMENT OF ALEXANDRIA, *STROMATEIS*, VI. VI (47)

"When it is said that 'the last enemy shall be destroyed,' it is not to be understood that his substance, which is God's creation, perishes, but that his purpose and hostile will perishes; for this does not come from God but from himself. Therefore his destruction means not his ceasing to exist but ceasing to be an enemy and ceasing to be death. Nothing is impossible to omnipotence; there is nothing that cannot be healed by its Maker; the Creator made all things in order that they might exist; and if things were made that they might exist they cannot become non-existent."

—ORIGEN, *DE PRINCIPIIS*, III. VI. 5

"The fabricator of the universe wanted to create man, not as a contemptible animal but as more honorable than all; so he brought him into being and appointed him king of the creation under heaven. Having decided this, and having endowed such a being with wise and godlike qualities and adorned him with much beauty, did he bring him into existence merely with the intention that once born he would perish and suffer complete annihilation?

That would surely be an idle goal, and it would be extremely improper to attribute such thinking to God. He then resembles small children who build enthusiastically and destroy as quickly their construction, which serves no useful purpose since their thought does not arrive at any useful achievement.

The doctrine we have received is quite the reverse. He created the firstformed man immortal, but when transgression and sin intruded he deprived him of immortality as a penalty for his fault. Then the fountain of goodness overflowed with kindness and turned in pity to the work of his own hands which he had adorned with wisdom and knowledge, and he was pleased to restore us to our ancient state."

—GREGORY OF NYSSA, *THE EASTER SERMONS OF GREGORY OF NYSSA*, 11

"And so our good Lord answered to all the questions and doubts which I could raise, saying most comfortingly: I may make all things well, and I shall make all things well, and I will make all things well; and you will see yourself that every kind of thing will be well."

—JULIAN OF NORWICH, *REVELATIONS OF DIVINE LOVE*, CHAPTER 31

"If sin must be kept alive, then hell must be kept alive; but while I regard the smallest sin as infinitely loathsome, I do not believe that any being, never good enough to see the essential ugliness of sin, could sin so as to deserve such punishment. I am not now, however, dealing with the question of the duration of punishment, but with the idea of punishment itself; and would only say in passing, that the notion that a creature born imperfect, nay, born with impulses to evil not of his own generating, and which he could not help having, a creature to whom the true face of God was never presented, and by whom it never could have been seen, should be thus condemned, is as loathsome a lie against God as could find place in a heart too undeveloped to understand what justice is, and too low to look up into the face of Jesus."

—GEORGE MACDONALD, "JUSTICE" IN *UNSPOKEN SERMONS SERIES III*

"God is not going to abandon creation, nor the people up for trial in criminal court, nor the Shiites, nor the communists, or the warmongers, nor the greedy and corrupt people in high places, nor the dope pushers, nor you, nor me. Bitter tears of repentance may be shed before we can join the celebration, but it won't be complete until we are all there."

—MADELEINE L'ENGLE, *A STONE FOR A PILLOW*, 58

"When we finally weary of our own selfishness, petty jealousies, and lust for power; when we learn at last, perhaps through bitter experience, that these lead only to a ruin and cannot bring enduring happiness, that nothing short of union with God and reconciliation with others will satisfy our own deepest yearnings; when we discover that the Hound of Heaven has finally closed off every alternative to such a union, we shall then, each of us, finally embrace the destiny that is ours."

—THOMAS TALBOTT, *THE INESCAPABLE LOVE OF GOD*, 225

"Christ did not die as he did to cancel an infinity of deserved punishment for humanity with the infinitely undeserved suffering of innocent divinity. The legal apparatus around the crucifixion is not there because God has a satisfaction case to prosecute and punishment to enforce on humanity, but because the machinery of false accusation and political and religious legitimacy are part of the way sacred violence works. The death of Jesus follows the script of human persecution because that is the ongoing evil into whose path Jesus steps, to rescue us from sacrifice, to open the way to new community."

—MARK HEIM, *SAVED FROM SACRIFICE*, 301.

"Love that is unrequited and ceases to love is not love at all. Love that demands reciprocity is not love at all. Love simply loves. And it loves whether the object of its desire returns its love or not. For us, when we reciprocate the love of the Father towards us, it's not about 'getting into heaven' or 'getting out of hell.' It's about the experience of a Father loving his child with all the love in his heart. There are no ulterior motives involved in the love of the Father for humanity. He is not seeking worshipers or workers. He is not looking for soldiers or servants. He is chasing his children, relentlessly, tenderly, endlessly. Whether we ever stop running and turn to face the light remains to be seen. Though I certainly hope that all will face the great light of the world and know as they are known, for now I remain at that point—in hope."

—CALEB MILLER, *SAVING GOD*, 231 32

"The people who know God well—the mystics, the hermits, those who risk everything to find God—always meet a lover, not a dictator. God is never found to be an abusive father or a tyrannical mother, but always a lover who is more than we dared hope for. How different from the 'accounting manager' that most people seem to worship. God is a lover who receives and forgives everything."

—RICHARD ROHR, *EVERYTHING BELONGS*, 131.

APPENDIX B
Could It Be... *the* Satan?

I wanted to include a very brief discussion on the satan, not necessarily to prove or disprove anything; but simply to put forth a succinct explanation of what I think he (or *it*) really is for those who don't quite buy into the "traditional" narrative. Nothing more, nothing less.[1] I'm certainly open to being dead wrong, as nothing we will explore here ultimately changes the theology I've introduced in these chapters. Perhaps this appendix only nuances things a bit.

First off, the satan literally means "the accuser." Considering Jesus labelled the satan a *liar* and a murderer from the beginning (John 8:44), one could expand on this a bit and describe the satan as a slanderer. Other definitions include, but are probably not limited to, "the adversary," "the tempter," "the executioner," and even "God's prosecuting attorney." Nevertheless, it is primarily a *role* or a *function* rather than a name or a person.

I know, I know, that's not what most of us have been taught. Indeed, we've no doubt heard that the satan more closely resembles a person rather than an overarching principle or something to that effect. (Using technical language, one could say he has his own ontology.) We read in the book of Job how the satan works as a field agent for the Lord. In fact, as Job 1:6 tells us, he is among the "heavenly beings;" his role being to walk around the earth and find people to levy accusations against.

So, it's obvious, the satan is a "person," right? And he works for God, right?

Well, hold on now. We don't have to be so literal. Some of this, I believe, is mythology and allegory. For instance, since we find cases where God himself is seen walking on the earth—as if God the Father is a person with actual legs—do we then capriciously make sweeping ontological claims that God is a literal bipedal being? Probably not. Moreover, there is also a whole history and development of thought that goes before Job and plays into this conversation about evil and its origins, which makes this whole discussion not so cut and dried.

Let's consider this now.

Essentially, thinking of a particular being who is the embodiment of evil began around 800 BCE, not with the ancient Hebrew people, but with this Persian dude named Zarathustra (his ideas lead to what is known as Zoroastrianism). In this tradition, two gods, nearly equal in power, are opposed against one another: the good spirit Spenta Mainyu and his twin brother Ahriman. After Israel's exile in sixth-century BCE, some of the Jewish people picked up some of the teachings of this tradition; one of them being the idea that there indeed was a being of pure evil. In this portion of the Hebrew tradition that Christianity later picked up on, however, the Zoroastrian doctrine gets a twist: the bad god is not really a god, but a fallen angel.

We've all heard how this tale goes:

> Satan starts off as a lovely angel. In fact, he's God's right-hand man. But then, as these things are wont to do, he not only rebels against God, but convinces a bunch of other angels to join

him in the uprising. Because of this, all of them are consigned to eternal torment. However, one of the angels strikes a deal with God, allowing one-third of them to stay on Earth for a time in order to corrupt humanity. In the end though, all the rebellious angels, Satan included, will be cast into hell to be burned for all eternity.

What is interesting is that this story isn't even a "biblical" one (unless you are Ethiopian Orthodox). You see, it comes from the book of Enoch, most specifically what is known as the book of the Watchers (1 Enoch 6–36). And yet, most of the Christianity I have experienced believes that the origins of evil come directly from this noncanonical tale. This is perplexing, so I would like to now offer an alternative to the "common" fallen angel myth, one that is more anthropological than theological. To do this, we'll begin by turning back to the book of Job.

The Satan as Human Community

Notice that after the first two chapters of Job, the mythological character named "Satan" vanishes. This is important because it means that for the next thirty-five chapters of the book, the principle of accusation will rest on the shoulders of humanity.

Here's how it all goes down.

After a host of terrible events befall the chief character, the community, intentions no doubt good, goes to work, clamoring on and on about how Job's illnesses and misfortunes are self-inflicted. Eliphaz warns that "those who plow iniquity and sow trouble reap the same" (Job 4:7–8); Bildad reminds Job that God will not "take the hand of evildoers" (Job 8:20); while Zophar implies that everything is Job's fault when he tells Job to "not let wickedness reside in your tents" (Job 11:14–15). Then, as the poems progress, the satanic momentum builds, and some even go so far as to create blatant falsities in order to condemn Job: that he takes clothing from the naked, that he has withheld water from the thirsty and bread from the hungry, and that he has turned away widows and crushed the arms of orphans (Job 22:6–7, 9).

The wicked truth about human community is that, even if our intentions start out as pure, we just can't help but devour our own. The book of Job testifies to this, even if it includes a bit of mythology in its prologue and epilogue. It testifies to the fact that when a community—indeed even so-called friends—turns against one of their own, they collectively become something more than the sum of their parts. In Job's story, each accuser is making individual charges, but the truth is that they are all a part of a larger whole that is being guided by what the writer, working within a particular historical context, can only call "Satan." In other words, as all the accusers come together as one, over against the "other," a mimetic monster is created, one that cannot help but demonize and devour Job, it's wretched scapegoat.

> The wicked truth about human community is that, even if our intentions start out as pure, we just can't help but devour our own.

The Satan as Twisted Desire

This human-centric understanding of evil is not only seen in Job 3–37, but also in the second creation story from the book of Genesis. Like the book of Job, there are mythological elements, one of which comes in the form of a talking serpent. This serpent, however, is obviously allegorical (snakes don't talk, do they?).

Here's my take on it.

As we discussed in chapter 3, human beings are imitative creatures. Our desires, rather than being instinctually fixed on predetermined objects, are picked up from the desires of others. There is beauty in this, but also great risk. When we desire what the other desires, we tend to get into rivalries for our shared objects of desire. Hence, as we go along in our lives, it becomes painfully obvious that certain prohibitions must be placed in order to quell the violence that will inevitably arise. The prohibition of the tree of knowledge of good and evil is a perfect example of this. In our quest to be just like God, to know all that is good and evil, we end up cannibalizing each other. And so, having this knowledge must be prohibited in order for us to have a chance to live in peace.

The problem, then, is that when something is prohibited, our desire for it grows ever stronger. One could say that prohibitions twist our desire, that they corrupt it. This is what the crafty serpent represents. Notice the corruption in the very first question asked of Eve: "Did God say, 'You shall not eat from any tree in the garden?'" (Gen 3:1) As we know, that is not what God said. There is only one prohibited tree, not many. This is a trap. Sure, Eve initially corrects the serpent, but she then imitates it by making up her own lie. It's subtle, but it's there, plain as day. She answers: "You shall not eat of the fruit of the tree that is in the middle of the garden, *nor shall you touch it*, or you shall die"

(Gen 3:3, emphasis mine). So, what began with one prohibition has now been twisted into two.

Initially, however, nothing happens to Eve. It is only after the man—who was there with her the whole time—eats of the fruit that both of their eyes are opened. This suggests that all three of the characters—the serpent, Eve, and Adam—are connected in a certain way. Michael Hardin points out that: "All of this literarily suggests that the man, the woman and the serpent are one big figure of the process of mediated desire and its consequences."[2] What are these consequences? Initially, accusations and scapegoating: the man blames both God and the woman (Gen 3:12), then the woman follows by turning it back onto the serpent (Gen 3:13).

The story goes on, and more consequences follow. What begins with a lie in chapter 3 quickly turns into a murder in chapter 4. In his grasping for God's blessing, Cain kills Abel. Brother rises up against brother. Then, Cain founds a city; civilization built upon blood. From there, violence escalates until the whole world is corrupt and full of wickedness.

Consider that this is what is what is meant when Jesus calls the satan a "liar and a murderer from the beginning." Satan is not some fallen angel who at one point was God's consigliere. Satan is and always has been pure evil. The scary part, however, is that the satan is a part of us. That is to say, the satan has its ontology in humanity. We are the ones who engage in lies (Gen 3). We are the ones who found our cultures and civilizations on murder (Gen 4). We are the ones who accuse and scapegoat others when their lives end up in ruin (the poems from Job). And we are the ones who have been doing this ever since.

In Closing

What I want to emphasize is that while the satan is human, it is always more than about each individual. Indeed, it is more than the sum of its parts. It is a power and a force that seems to take on a life of its own, any time a group comes together in condemnation of an "other." Paul's phrase "the Powers and Principalities" seems like an apt way of describing it. And, as my friend Brad Jersak points out in the Beyond the Box Podcast, it is much worse than we tend to think.[3]

Yet, regardless if one finds my ontology of satan convincing or not, what we all should agree on is that the satan is a power that has been defeated by Christ. That's the promise of the New Testament. Does the satanic mechanism of accusing, scapegoating, and blaming continue? Of course. We live between the now and the not yet. This age hasn't passed on to the next; but it will, because we know at the end of all things, God will be all in all (1 Cor 15:28). In the meantime, whether we believe the satan is a dark lord with his own ontology, or whether we believe the satan is an allegory for a dark power or principle, we who live in the Spirit live a life void of accusations. We live a life oriented toward Love and Justice, and do our damnedest to bring more of both into a world so torn up by the satan.

> Whether we believe the satan is a dark lord with his own ontology, or whether we believe the satan is an allegory for a dark power or principle, we who live in the Spirit live a life void of accusations.

APPENDIX C

Paul's Universalism: A Brief Exegesis of Romans 5:12–19, 1 Corinthians 15:22–28, and Colossians 1:15–20

In chapter 8, I included three extended passages from Paul's writings that, on the surface, seem to argue for a salvation so corporate that all of humanity is included. This appendix, then, digs a little deeper into the passages at-hand and attempts to further solidify that a universalistic reading is the most appropriate one. (Note, the following is a snippet from my book, *From the Blood of Abel: Humanity's Root Causes of Violence and the Bible's Theological-Anthropological Solution.*)

Romans 5:12–19

"Therefore just as one man's trespass led to condemnation for all, so one man's act of righteousness leads to justification and life for all."

—ROM 5:18

In Romans 5:12, Paul begins with what appears to be an Aristotelian logical sequence. He states:

1. Adam's sin lead to death.

2. All have sinned.

3. Therefore, death spread to all people.

In this progression, Adam is viewed as a corporate figure, as he is directly attached to the sin and death every human being experiences. Notice, then, that in verse 14, Paul intentionally makes a parallel between Adam and Christ when he says that Adam is a type of "the one who was to come." So, like Adam, Christ is envisioned as a corporate figure. Now, although Adam and Christ are paralleled, Paul then argues in verse 15 that what Christ offers, namely a free gift, is going to be different than what Adam brought to all, which of course was sin and death. In fact, Paul will go on in that verse to weigh the free gift as "much more" than the sin and death Adam introduced into the world. I will note that what Paul is doing here is employing something called *argumentum a fortiori*, which seems to be a forerunner to a rabbinic hermeneutical method called "ka-va-chomer."[1] When he does this, it is to place emphasis on the thing that is "much more," namely the second clause that naturally follows from the first. In this case, that which is "much more" is the free gift of grace.

We should not fail to notice that in verse 15, the language to describe those who sinned and those who receive grace is slightly dissimilar to verse 12. Instead of using the more inclusive sounding "all," Paul uses the word "many," but again makes a strong parallel between Adam's sin and Christ's grace. Sin and death abounds to "many"—which, unless Paul is contradicting himself, is in fact all—but how *much more* does the grace of Christ abound to that very same "many."

In verse 18, Paul concludes his argument stating, "Therefore just as one man's trespass led to condemnation for all, so one man's act of righteousness leads to justification and life for all." Now, some may point back to Paul's use of the word *lambanó* in verse 17, and argue that one must actively "receive" Christ's grace in order to "be saved." However, this interpretation has three problems.

- First, when thinking about Paul's Damascus road event, what did Paul actively do with regards to *receiving* Christ's grace? If you may recall, it was Christ who blinded him, Christ who confronted his persecution, and then Christ through Ananias who welcomes Paul into the "Christian" community. Remember, it is Ananias' "brother Saul" that causes the scales to fall from Paul's eyes. Therefore, did Paul *really* have a choice as to whether he would receive this grace?

- The second issue with this interpretation of "receive" is that one would have to take a single verse—actually, a single word—out of the overall thrust of Paul's argument from vv. 12–19. That is to say, setting both Adam and Christ up as paralleled corporate figures seems irresponsible if Adam's death affects a greater number of humans than Christ's free gift of grace (as many Christians contend there will be those who do not actively receive it).

- Lastly, throughout Paul's writings, when he uses the Greek verb *lambanó* in conjunction with a divine gift of some kind, the receiver is always passive.[2] Philosopher Thomas Talbott puts forth these examples: "When Paul declared, 'five times I have received (active voice)…the forty lashes minus one' (2 Cor 11:24), we understand that he received these thirty-nine lashes in the same passive sense that a boxer might receive severe blows to the head; and when he spoke of those who 'have received (active voice) grace and apostleship to bring about the obedience of faith,' (Rom 1:5), we again understand that such persons are the recipients of some divine action in the same passive way that a newborn baby receives life."[3]

So, given the evidence—Paul's firsthand conversion experience as well as the self-evident tenor of the argument he presents in vv. 12–19—we would have to conclude that throughout this passage, *all* means *all*, all of the time. Thus, just as one man (Adam) caused all to sin and die, so too will one man (Christ) give life to *all*.

1 Corinthians 15:22-28

"For as all die in Adam, so all will be made alive in Christ."

—1 COR 15:22

Quite similar to Romans 5:18, Paul, starting in 1 Corinthians 15:22, again makes a parallel between the corporate figures Adam and Christ—"a man from the earth" and "a man of heaven" respectively (1 Cor 15:47). 1 Corinthians 15:22 reads: "For as all die in Adam, so all will be made alive in Christ." In vv. 23–24, Paul goes on to flesh out the details of how this will happen, "But each in his own order: Christ the first fruits, then at his coming those who belong to Christ. Then comes the end, when he hands over the kingdom to God the Father, after he has destroyed every ruler and every authority and power." Talbott interprets this passage in the following manner:

> After informing us that "in Christ shall all be made alive," Paul went on to say, "But each in his own order" (v 23). It is as if he had in mind the image of a procession and then quickly listed three segments of the procession. At the head of the procession is Christ, the first fruits; behind him are those who belong to Christ at the time of his coming; and behind him are those at the end of the procession, which is the third and final stage of Paul's "each in his own order."[4]

This was also how I interpreted this passage in *All Set Free*. And while I believe it is a solid interpretation, I now tend to lean toward an alternate one, namely one that interprets the processional as follows: Christ the first fruits, those who belong to Christ (the same everybody that are in Adam), then the end, which is when Christ destroys all rulers, authorities, and powers. That is to say, everyone in Christ is made alive (1 Cor 15:22) and then Christ will destroy the very concept of rulership, as all authority and power is Christ's and Christ's only. Then death itself—which stems from the violent systems of power—is destroyed in 1 Corinthians 15:26.

So, what does Paul mean when he mentions "death?"

When talking about death, Paul does so in two paradoxical sounding ways. First, in one sense, Romans 6:6–7 tells us that we must die in order to be freed from sin. Yet, in Romans 7:9–10, Paul says that he died once sin was revived. In other words, according to Paul, death (to your own fleshy desires) delivers you from sin but (in a spiritual sense) is the consequence of sin.

So, when death, the last enemy, is destroyed, it is done for two distinct reasons.

1. The very thing we all need to do in order to live is to die to ourselves. Once we all do this, we no longer need death as a means by which we find life.

2. When we all die to ourselves and indeed find life in Christ, death, the final enemy, will be destroyed because life in Christ is eternal.

And so, only after death itself is destroyed—that is to say, once the only thing that can keep us from God is done away with—the Son will subject even himself to the Father so that God "may be all in all" (1 Cor 15:28). Not *all* in some or *all* in what's left, but *all* in *all*.

Colossians 1:15–20

"Through him God was pleased to reconcile to himself all things."

—COL 1:20

Colossians 1:15–20 is a part of an early Christian hymn—a triumphant declaration.

> He is the image of the invisible God, the firstborn of *all* creation; for in him *all* things in heaven and on earth were created, things visible and invisible, whether thrones or dominions or rulers or powers—*all* things have been created through him and for him. He himself is before *all* things, and in him *all* things hold together. He is the head of the body, the church; he is the beginning, the firstborn from the dead, so that he might come

to have first place in *everything*. For in him *all* the fullness of God was pleased to reconcile to himself *all* things, whether on earth or in heaven, by making peace through the blood of his cross. (emphasis mine)

In this passage, Paul again uses strong, inclusive language when describing the scope of Christ's reign. Similar to 1 Corinthians 15:24, in Colossians 1:16 Paul even declares all "thrones, dominions, rulers, or powers" as subjected to Christ. Even these "powers and principalities" that spilled Jesus' blood—and in fact have been shedding the blood of all the prophets "since the foundation of the world"—are included in the "all things" that are reconciled to him (Col 1:20).

And how are "all things" reconciled to God?

Paul offers us a glimpse: "by making peace through the blood of his cross" (Col 1:20). Remember, the peace of Jesus is pervasive throughout the gospels and is central to Paul's teaching as well. In fact, in Ephesians 6:15, the Gospel is called a "gospel of peace." For Paul, peace is the reconciliatory agent that unites humankind with God. And that peace was only possible because Jesus was the embodiment of such peace. So, he is then given the name above all names and will come to have first place in everything (Col 1:18). Not some things or all things that are left, but *all* things.

Concluding Remarks

I will close by emphasizing the importance in noticing the consistency in Paul's language throughout the three letters we discussed. In Romans 5:12–19, Christ is paralleled with Adam and, in fact, offers a gift that is "much more" than what Adam offered.

Adam brought sin and death, but Christ brings righteousness and life. This point is driven home again in 1 Corinthians 15:22 (as well as Philippians 2:5–11). What I believe Paul is trying to say is that whatever was done in Adam, was in the same way— nay, in a way *much greater*—undone by Christ. The Gospel, then, according to Paul, is not about what has to be done, but about what has already been done. For all of us.

APPENDIX D

Universal Reconciliation: A Compilation of New Testament Passages

LUKE 3:5–6

Every valley shall be filled, and every mountain and hill shall be made low, and the crooked shall be made straight, and the rough ways made smooth; and all flesh shall see the salvation of God.

JOHN 3:17

Indeed, God did not send the Son into the world to condemn the world, but in order that the world might be saved through him.

JOHN 12:32

And I, when I am lifted up from the earth, will draw all people to myself.

JOHN 17:2

Since you have given him authority over all people, to give eternal life to all whom you have given him.

ACTS 3:19-21

Repent therefore, and turn to God so that your sins may be wiped out, so that times of refreshing may come from the presence of the Lord, and that he may send the Messiah appointed for you, that is, Jesus, who must remain in heaven until the time of universal restoration that God announced long ago through his holy prophets.

ROMANS 5:18-19

Therefore just as one man's trespass led to condemnation for all, so one man's act of righteousness leads to justification and life for all. For just as by the one man's disobedience the many were made sinners, so by the one man's obedience the many will be made righteous.

ROMANS 11:30-32

Just as you were once disobedient to God but have now received mercy because of their obedience, so they have now been disobedient in order that, by the mercy shown to you, they too may now receive mercy. For God has imprisoned all in disobedience so that he may be merciful to all.

ROMANS 14:11

As I live, says the Lord, every knee shall bow to me, and every tongue shall give praise to God.

1 CORINTHIANS 15:22

For as all die in Adam, so all will be made alive in Christ.

1 CORINTHIANS 15:28

When all things are subjected to him, then the Son himself will also be subjected to the one who put all things in subjection under him, so that God may be all in all.

2 CORINTHIANS 5:18-19

All this is from God, who reconciled us to himself through Christ, and has given us the ministry of reconciliation; that is, in Christ God was reconciling the world to himself, not counting their trespasses against them, and entrusting the message of reconciliation to us.

EPHESIANS 1:9-10

He has made known to us the mystery of his will, according to his good pleasure that he set forth in Christ, as a plan for the fullness of time, to gather up all things in him, things in heaven and things on earth.

PHILIPPIANS 2:9-11

Therefore God also highly exalted him and gave him the name that is above every name, so that at the name of Jesus every knee should bend, in heaven and on earth and under the earth, and every tongue should confess that Jesus Christ is Lord, to the glory of God the Father.

COLOSSIANS 1:19-20

For in him all the fullness of God was pleased to dwell, and through him God was please to reconcile to himself all things, whether on earth or in heaven, by making peace through the blood of his cross.

1 TIMOTHY 2:3-4

This is right and acceptable in the sight of God our Savior, who desires everyone to be saved and to come to the knowledge of the truth.

1 TIMOTHY 4:10

For to this end we toil and struggle, because we have our hope set on the living God, who is the Savior of all people, especially of those who believe.

TITUS 2:11–13

For the grace of God has appeared, bringing salvation to all, training us to renounce impiety and worldly passions, and in the present age to live lives that are self-controlled, upright, and godly, while we wait for the blessed hope and the manifestation of the glory of our great God and Savior, Jesus Christ.

1 JOHN 2:1–2

If anyone does sin, we have an advocate with the Father, Jesus Christ the righteous; and he is the atoning sacrifice for our sins, and not for ours only but also for the sins of the whole world.

REVELATION 5:13

Then I heard every creature in heaven and on earth and under the earth and in the sea, and all that is in them, singing, "To the one seated on the throne and to the Lamb be blessing and honor and glory and might forever and ever!"

REVELATION 21:3–4

See, the home of God is among mortals. He will dwell with them; they will be his peoples, and God himself will be with them; he will wipe every tear from their eyes. Death will be no more; mourning and crying and pain will be no more, for the first things have passed away.

End Notes

INTRODUCTION
1. Hardin, "Finding Our Way Home," para. 48.

CHAPTER 1
1. Piper, "Universalism and the Reality of Eternal Punishment," para. 29.
2. Jordan, "Universalism vs the Gospel," para 3.
3. Ross, "Donald Trump," para. 1–2.
4. For a deeper look into the potential cataclysmic effects of our current self-destructive ways, both René Girard (*Battling to the End*) and Jean-Pierre Dupuy (*The Mark of the Sacred*) offer in-depth surveys that I highly recommend.
5. See https://www.armscontrol.org/factsheets/Nuclearweaponswhohaswhat.
6. This passage is, admittedly, a textual variant, and is not found in the original Greek manuscripts. However, it certainly does follow the spirit of Jesus' teachings on forgiveness that are found littered all throughout the gospels.
7. This is the point John's Gospel is trying to make by having Jesus' death on Thursday rather than Friday, as the Synoptics (Matthew, Mark, and Luke) have it. The writer of the Fourth Gospel places Jesus' death at the same exact time the Passover lamb was to be slaughtered in the Temple in order to subvert the "traditional" notion of sacrifice. In essence, what is being conveyed is that while the priests were making sacrifices inside the city, the true sacrifice was slain outside the city, on a hill called

Golgotha. For a detailed look at the subversive nature of Jesus' sacrificial death, see James Alison's essay "God's Self-Substitution and Sacrificial Inversion" in *Stricken by God? Nonviolent Identification and the Victory of Christ*. Edited by Jersak and Hardin. Grand Rapids: Eerdmans, 2007.

8. Becker, Ernest. *The Denial of Death*. New York: Free Press, 1973.

9. In no way do I mean this as a slight against atheists (I myself was one), but as a historical fact.

10. Tacitus, *Annals*, Book XV, Ch. 44.

11. Ibid.

12. The term "Logos" comes from, among other places, John 1:1–5. It is a Greek word that most of our English bibles translate as "Word." But it is much more than just speech. In fact, prior to Socrates, Heraclitus argued that the Logos was that which structures the entire world. Incidentally, he also argued that that structural principle is violence. The counter to this is, of course, the nonviolent Logos of Christ which John talks of. Instead of a Logos of war and strife (Heraclitus, fragments 53 and 80), the true Logos is imbued with love, grace, and peace.

13. This is the very first time the word "sin" is mentioned in the Hebrew Bible.

14. Girard, "Are the Gospels Mythical?," para. 10.

CHAPTER 2

1. Slick, "The Elements of Liberalism," sec. II, para. 5.

2. Morrow, "Beware of Progressive Christianity," para. 10.

3. The KJV actually gets this correct, and reads "And all bare him witness." However, most translations, such as the NRSV and NIV, tell us that all "spoke well of Jesus."

4. Hardin, *Jesus Driven Life*, 67.

5. Ibid., 70.

6. Ibid., 69–70.

7. Girard, *I See Satan*, 14.

8. What Jesus is not saying is that Christians are to allow themselves and others to be persecuted. Regarding Jesus' command to non-resistance, Michael Hardin points out, "The Greek verb used (*antistenai*) does not mean be a doormat, it means that when you are abused (persecuted), you 'speak truth to power' by engaging in actions which, while nonviolent, are also resistant. Turning the other cheek does not mean letting someone strike you over and over. It is a way of calling attention to the abuse in a nonviolent fashion such that the abuser will recognize the futility of their actions." (Hardin, *Jesus Driven Life*, 126) See, also, Walter Wink's *Engaging the Powers*, pp 175–77.

9. Enns, *The Bible Tells Me So*, 176.

10. From an interview with *Relevant Magazine* that can be found at http://www.relevantmagazine.com/god/church/features/1344-from-the-mag-7-big-questions.

11. Martyn, *Galatians*, 246–47.

12. Evidence for this can be found in Romans 1:18–32, as well as Galatians 5:19–21. In both instances, Paul is rhetorically playing the role of the false teacher and quotes traditional anti-Gentile rhetoric that can be found in Wisdom of Solomon 13–14, but in other places as well. (Campbell, *Deliverance*, 360–62)

13. Martyn, *Galatians*, 364–70.

14. Those who come to mind include, but are not limited to, J. Louis Martyn and Chris Tilling.

15. Campbell, *Deliverance*, 587.

16. Martyn, *Galatians*, 364–70.

CHAPTER 3

1. Mann, "Myth of a Non-Violent Jesus," para. 11.

2. Williams, *Being Christian*, 38.

3. Hamerton-Kelly, *Violent Origins*, 141.

4. Girard, *I See Satan*, 137.

5. Ibid., 15.

6. Ibid., 9.

7. When I suggest that Bin Laden was a scapegoat, I am not saying he was innocent of the crimes he committed, or that he was a "good person," or anything to that effect. In all likelihood, he was a very evil man. However, one's morality has nothing to do with the scapegoating mechanism. In the eyes of a society in crisis, the scapegoat is guilty of everything *they* say he is guilty of, which is, not coincidently, almost always the very ills the society is suffering through. While it is easy to point out how evil Bin Laden was, and how much responsibility he bore for some of the atrocities in the Middle East and elsewhere, his killing achieved nothing in addressing the underlying problems that still remain. In fact, only more "bin Ladens" continue to rise up, in large part because of the hegemonic foreign policy of the West, and more specifically the United States.

8. Admittedly, the details regarding the Maria Lionzan religion are speculative at best. As Gabriel Ernesto Andrade writes, "It is impossible to speak about any aspect of Maria Lionzan religion with certainty. There are no official beliefs and practices, there are no canons. Historians have not been able to reach an agreement as to when and how this religion started to develop." (Andrade, "A Girardian Reading," sec. 1, para. 1)

9. Ibid., sec. 5, para. 26–33.

10. Girard, *I See Satan*, 79.

11. Alison, *Knowing Jesus*, 33–58.

12. Hardin, *Jesus Driven Life*, 175.

CHAPTER 4

1. Dyer, "The God of the Old and New Testaments," para. 7.

2. Nelson, "Marcion Lives!" para. 4.

3. Hamack, *History of Dogma,* vol. 1, ch. 5, 271.

4. In all reality, it is henotheistic/monolatrous, as Marcion recognized the creator God as a separate deity, but worshipped only one God, namely the Abba of Jesus.

5. For a more historically accurate picture of the Pharisees, as well as the other Second Temple sects, see Stephen M. Wylen's *The Jews in the Time of Jesus: An Introduction*. New York: Paulist, 1996, 133–47.

6. See Luther's Heidelberg Disputation of 1518, most specifically theses 19–21.

7. Hardin, *What the Facebook?*, 152

8. Ibid., 152–53.

CHAPTER 5

1. Slick, "What does the Bible say," para. 2.

2. This quote can be found at https://www.compellingtruth.org/gay-marriage.html.

3. These verses include Genesis 19; Leviticus 18:22, 20:13; Romans 1:26–27; 1 Corinthians 6:9–10; 1 Timothy 1:9–10; Jude 1:7.

4. Quoted in Hardin, *What the Facebook?*, 232.

5. Regarding Leviticus 20:13, my good friend and Hebrew scholar, Mark Stone, in a recent Facebook conversation, reminded me that: "The only two explicit proscriptions against homosexual behavior are found in Leviticus 18:22 and 20:13, and they are not nearly as far-reaching as many have supposed. The two texts condemn 'lying with a male as with a woman.' Leviticus 20:13 specifically forbids that a 'male' (*'ish*) have sex with a 'male' (*zachar*). This is curious, as the two words both mean a generic male. Why use the different vocabulary? The best way to understand the curious shift in vocabulary is to read it in the broader context (this also applies to 18:22). Essentially, the use of *zachar* is to clarify that all the 'male versions' of sexual abominations enumerated in the previous (and likely forthcoming) verses are also proscribed. Ergo, the homosexual prohibition applies to sex with father, son, and brother and to grandfather-grandson, uncle-nephew, and stepfather-stepson, but—and this is the crucial bit—not to male-male sexual intercourse in general. To make such a claim is blatant eisegesis, not to mention grossly anachronistic. This applies mutatis mutandis to female-female as well."

6. Corey, "For the People Who Say," para. 7.

7. Hornblower and Spawforth, *Oxford Classical Dictionary*, 720.

8. I'll note that if Pauline scholar Douglas Campbell is correct, Romans 1:26–27 is a portion of the "false teachers'" argument Paul is dead set on rebuking, beginning in Romans 2:1. See Campbell's *The Deliverance of God: An Apocalyptic Rereading of Justification in Paul*. Grand Rapids: Eerdmans, 2009

9. Shore, *Unfair*, 9 I will also note that in *Paul Among the People: The Apostle Reinterpreted and Reimagined in His Own Time*, Sarah Ruden makes a strong case that whenever Paul discusses "homosexuality," it is in the context that pederasty was running rampant in the Greco-Roman world.

10. This is assuming Paul wrote 1 Timothy. Scholars tend to be divided. For our purposes, it matters not.

11. The KJV gets this right and translates "malakoi" as "effeminate."

12. Giles, "Is it a Sin?," para. 62–64. (Cf. Plato, *The Republic*, Book III; Josephus, *Wars of the Jews*, 7.338; Aristotle, *Nicomachean Ethics*, 7.4.4.)

13. From the *New American Bible (Revised Edition)*, footnote b, 1 Corinthians 6:9.

14. MacArthur, *MacArthur New Testament Commentary*, 146.

15. Giles, "Is it a Sin?," para. 55. (Cf. Philo, *The Special Laws*, III, VII, 40–42.)

16. The claim that Paul was radically inclusive will no doubt be disputed. So, for a detailed look at how I read Paul's letters, see the following: *Galatians* by J. Louis Martyn, and *The Deliverance of God: An Apocalyptic Rereading of Justification in Paul* by Douglas Campbell. For my money, these two books are *the* game changers in the world of Pauline studies.

CHAPTER 6

1. Olson, "How serious a heresy is universalism?," para. 9.

2. From an interview with filmmaker Kevin Miller that can be viewed in full at https://vimeo.com/110259939.

3. Augustine, *Enchiridion*, sec. 112.

4. Ramelli, *Christian Doctrine*, 11.

5. Ibid.

6. See Acts 3:19–21, which reads, "Repent therefore, and turn to God so that your sins may be wiped out, so that times of refreshing may come from the presence of the Lord, and that he may send the Messiah appointed for you, that is, Jesus, who must remain in heaven until the time of universal restoration [*apokatastasis*] that God announced long ago through his holy prophets."

7. Ramelli, *Christian Doctrine*, 11.

8. Ludlow, "Universalism in the History of Christianity," 195.

9. To see the difference between the earliest Greek version and the later Latin one, see Hanson, *Universalism*, Ch. 1, para. 5.

10. Hanson, *Universalism*, 133.

11. Augustine, *Confessions*, 15.

12. Ibid., 17.

13. Hanson, *Universalism*, 274.

14. Ibid., 273.

15. Barclay, *New Testament Words*, 37.

16. Marshall, *Beyond Retribution*, 186.

17. All quotes can be found at http://www.tentmaker.org/Quotes/churchfathersquotes.htm.

CHAPTER 7

1. Slick, "Substitutionary Atonement," sec. II, para. 7.

2. DeYoung, "Substitution," para. 7.

3. Alison, "God's Self-Substitution," 168–69. Alison expands on this notion throughout his essay, writing: "Now, here's the interesting point: for the Temple understanding, the high priest at this stage was acting 'in the person of Yahweh,' and it was the Lord's blood that was being sprinkled. This was a divine movement to set people free. It was not—as we often imagine—a priest satisfying a divinity. The reason why the priest had to engage in a prior expiation was that he was about to

become a sign of something quite the opposite; he was acting outwards. The movement is not inwards into the Holy of Holies; the movement is outwards from the Holy of Holies." (Ibid., 169)

4. See, for instance, the First Council of Nicaea (325 BCE) and the Athanasian Creed (date unknown).

5. There is a hilarious video from "ReligiontoReason" that shows what it would be like if we forgave in the same way the penal substitution folks say God forgives. It can be found at https://www.youtube.com/watch?v=fTiBdmJ-PuE.

6. Cf. Anselm's *Cur Deus Homo* (1098).

7. Clement, *The Exhortation to the Greeks*, 346.

8. Distefano and Machuga, *Journey*, 43–44.

9. Beck, *Slavery of Death*, 41–42.

10. Ibid., xii.

11. Hamerton-Kelly, *The Gospel*, 44.

CHAPTER 8

1. Lewis, *Great Divorce*, 73.

2. Sanders, "A Freewill Theist's Response," 180.

3. Lewis, *Problem of Pain*, 127.

4. Augustine, *Confessions*, 7.

5. Calvin, *Institutes*, 3.17.5.

6. Ibid.

7. Hart, "God, Creation, and Evil," 7.

8. Ibid., 8.

9. Distefano and Machuga, *Journey*, 79.

10. Thomas, "William Perkins," para. 4.

11. The term for this system of thinking is "experiential predestinarianism."

12. Patton, "Doubting Calvinists," para. 16.
13. Ibid.
14. Kant, *Religion*, 19.
15. Machuga, *Three Theological Mistakes*, 181.
16. Hart, "God, Creation, and Evil," 10.
17. Tolkien, *Fellowship of the Ring*, 472.
18. Williams, *Mere Humanity*, 124–25.
19. Barth, *Church Dogmatics* II.2, 779.
20. Talbott, "Toward a Better Understanding of Universalism," 5.
21. Walls, *Hell*, 129–138.
22. Reitan, "Human Freedom," 134.
23. Hart, "God, Creation, and Evil," 10.
24. Girard, *I See Satan*, 15.
25. Girard, *Things Hidden*, Book III.
26. Hart, "God, Creation, and Evil," 10.
27. The Greek verb *helko*, which gets translated to "draw," also implies "dragging or pulling."
28. For a fairly detailed exegesis of the following passages, see Appendix C, as well as *All Set Free*, pp. 81–88, *From the Blood of Abel*, pp. 165–78, and my essay, "Paul's Inclusive Theology," which can be found at http://www.allsetfree.com/wp-content/uploads/2016/03/Pauls-inclusive-theology-final.pdf.
29. This is assuming Paul in fact wrote Colossians. Scholars are divided on whether he did or not. For our purposes, it matters not.

CHAPTER 9

1. Piper, "God's Wrath," sec. 2, para. 7.
2. This definition can be found at http://www.studylight.org/dictionaries/ctd/w/wrath.html.

3. Edwards, *The Works*, 458.

4. Romans 2:5; 4:15; 5:9; 9:22; 12:19; 13:4–5.

5. Jersak, *A More Christlike God*, 209–10.

CHAPTER 10

1. From an interview with *Relevant Magazine* that can be found at http://www.relevantmagazine.com/god/church/features/1344-from-the-mag-7-big-questions.

2. See Revelation 3:5; 20:12.

3. Bickle, "Armageddon Campaign," 4.

4. The phrase "caught up in the clouds" comes from Daniel 7:13–14, and is echoed by Paul in 1 Thessalonians 4:15–17. On the surface, one could assume these texts—in English at least—argue for a Rapture of the Church, in which believers leave this evil earthly realm to be caught up in the clouds with the Lord. However, that would be to approach the passages at-hand outside of their original context. How so? First, the clouds of heaven Daniel 7:13 and 1 Thessalonians 4:17 mentioned are in regards to Jesus' "coming upward in vindication," as N.T. Wright puts it (Wright, *Surprised by Scripture*, 101). In other words, it is a subversive claim about where true authority and power come from (Isa 52:13–15), not one about some snatching away of an elect group to some parallel universe in the sky. Second, when Paul uses the Greek word *apantesis*, or "to meet," he is using it in the context of how citizens of a town in that day would have greeted a high-ranking official with the goal of ushering him *into* their city. That is to say, when the people "meet up" with the official, they don't leave, they bring him in. Again, here is Wright on the connection: "The point is that Jesus will reign on the earth, and at his royal appearing the faithful will go to meet him, like the disciples on the road to Jerusalem only now in full-blooded triumph, and escort him *back into the world* that is rightfully his and that he comes to claim, to judge, to rule with healing and wise sovereignty" (Ibid., 102, emphasis mine).

5. Wright, *Surprised by Scripture*, 84.

6. Jersak, "I Saw a Lamb," 328.

7. To strengthen the case for this Christotelic interpretation of "the end," Brad Jersak notices: "Remember, if the book of Revelation is sourced in the same community as the Gospel of John, the Cross *is* the throne on which Christ is lifted up as judge to render eschatological judgement… thus…viewed through the Gospel lens, Revelation 12 understands the victory of the Lamb and his 'armies' as a triumph through their martyr witness—past and future—rather than some neo-zealot reversion to violence by Rambo-Jesus and his special forces. Whatever form the *parousia* will take, it will be consistent with the Way of the Lamb (think 'Sermon on the Mount') and a consummation of the New Covenant of Christ's saving, forgiving blood." (Jersak, "I Saw a Lamb," 317)

8. Jersak, "I Saw a Lamb," 318.

9. Ibid., 320.

APPENDIX B

1. For those interested in digging deeper into this topic, see *The Satan* by Michael Hardin (https://preachingpeace.org/the-satan/), *I See Satan Fall Like Lightning* by René Girard, *The Slavery of Death* by Richard Beck, and *Desire Found Me* by Andre Rabe.

2. Hardin, "The Satan," sec. 11.

3. The interview I'm referring to can be heard at http://www.beyondtheboxpodcast.com/2013/02/the-satan-with-michael-hardin-and-brad-jersak/.

APPENDIX C

1. Hardin, "Romans 5:12–21," 2.

2. Talbott, *Inescapable Love of God*, 58.

3. Ibid.

4. Ibid., 61.

Bibliography

Alison, James. "God's Self-Substitution and Sacrificial Inversion." In Jersak and Hardin, eds. *Stricken by God?: Nonviolent Identification and the Victory of Christ.* Grand Rapids: Eerdmans, 2007.

Andrade, Gabriel Ernesto. "A Girardian Reading of the Myth of Maria Lionza." *AnthroBase.* http://www.anthrobase.com/Txt/A/Andrade_G_E_01.htm.

Augustine. *Confessions.* Translated by Henry Chadwick. Oxford: Oxford University Press, 1991.

———. *Confessions and Enchiridion.* Translated and edited by Albert C. Outler. Philadelphia: Westminster Press, 1955.

Barclay, William. *New Testament Words.* Louisville: Westminster John Knox, 1964.

Barth, Karl. *Church Dogmatics.* Translated by G.W. Bromiley, G.T. Thompson, and Harold Knight. London: T&T Clark, 2009.

Bettenson, Henry, ed. *The Early Christian Fathers: A section from the writings of the Fathers from St. Clement of Rome to St. Athanasius.* Oxford: Oxford University Press, 1956.

Bickle, Mike. "Armageddon Campaign: The Battle of the Great Day of God Almighty." *Forerunner School of Ministry* (March 2006). http://www.mikebickle.org.edgesuite.net/MikeBickleVOD/2006/20060304-T-Armageddon_and_the_Second_Coming_of_Christ.pdf.

Campbell, Douglas. *The Deliverance of God: An Apocalyptic Rereading of Justification in Paul.* Grand Rapids: Eerdmans, 2009.

Chalker, William Houston. *Calvin and Some Seventeenth Century English Calvinists: A Comparison of their Thought Through an Examination of their Doctrines of Knowledge of God, Faith, and Assurance.* Durham: Duke University Press, 1961.

Clement. *The Exhortation to the Greeks.* Translated by G.W. Butterworth. Cambridge: Harvard University Press, 1960.

Corey, Benjamin L. "For the People Who Say, 'But Jesus Didn't Abolish the Law.'" *Formerly Fundie.* (August 2015). http://www.patheos.com/blogs/formerlyfundie/for-the-people-who-say-but-jesus-didnt-abolish-the-law/.

DeYoung, Kevin. "Substitution is Not a 'Theory of the Atonement." *The Gospel Coalition* (March 2016). https://blogs.thegospelcoalition.org/kevindeyoung/2016/03/22/substitution-is-not-a-theory-of-the-atonement/.

Distefano, Matthew J. *From the Blood of Abel: Humanity's Root Causes of Violence and the Bible's Theological-Anthropological Solution.* Orange: Quoir, 2016.

Distefano, Matthew J., and Machuga, Michael. *A Journey with Two Mystics: Conversations between a Girardian and a Wattsian.* Eugene: Resource, 2017.

Doherty, Lillian E. *Gender and the Interpretation of Classical Myth.* London: Bloomsbury, 2003.

Dyer, Billy. "The God of the Old and New Testaments; Same or Different?" *DyerThoughts* (February 2015). http://www.dyerthoughts.com/home/the-god-of-the-old-new-testaments-same-or-different.

Edwards, Jonathan. *The Works of President Edwards.* New York: Burt Franklin, 1968.

Enns, Peter. *The Bible Tells Me So: Why Defending Scripture has made us Unable to Read It.* New York: HarperOne, 2014.

Furman, Richard. "Exposition of the Views of the Baptists, Relative to the Colored Population in the United States: In Communication to the Governor of South Carolina." Second ed. Charleston, 1838. http://eweb.furman.edu/~benson/docs/rcd-fmn1.htm.

Garrels, Scott R. "Imitation, Mirror Neurons, and Mimetic Desire: Convergence between the Mimetic Theory of René Girard and Empirical Research on Imitation." *Contagion: Journal of Violence, Mimesis, and Culture* 12–13 (2006) 47–86. http://static1.squarespace.com/static/55a55b50e4b08015467323fc/t/565f4a92e4b0a6f556b4e7c4/1449085586674/Contagion_12-13_Garrels_47-86.pdf.

Giles, Keith. "Is it a Sin to be Gay?" *Patheos* (January 2018). http://www.patheos.com/blogs/keithgiles/2018/01/is-it-a-sin-to-be-gay/.

Girard, René. "Are the Gospels Mythical?" *First Things* (April 1996). https://www.firstthings.com/article/1996/04/are-the-gospels-mythical.

———. *I See Satan Fall like Lightning*. Translated by James G. Williams. New York: Orbis, 2001.

———. *Things Hidden Since the Foundation of the World*. Translated by Stephen Bann and Michael Metteer. Stanford: Stanford University Press, 1978.

Hamerton-Kelly, Robert. *The Gospel and the Sacred: Poetics of Violence in Mark*. Minneapolis: Augsburg Fortress, 1994.

Hamerton-Kelly, Robert, ed. *Violent Origins: Ritual Killing and Cultural Foundation*. Stanford: Stanford University Press, 1987.

Hanson, J.W. *Universalism: The Prevailing Doctrine of the Christian Church During Its First Five Hundred Years*. Boston and Chicago: Universalist, 1899.

Hardin, Michael. "Finding Our Way Home: A Brief Note on the Authority and Interpretation of Scripture." *Preaching Peace* (December 2003). http://www.preachingpeace.org/news/26-articles-ebooks/articles-ebooks-by-michael-hardin/92-finding-our-way-home-a-brief-note-on-the-authority-and-interpretation-of-scripture.html.

———. *The Jesus Driven Life: Reconnecting Humanity with Jesus*. 2nd Edition. Lancaster: JDL, 2013.

———. "Romans 5:12–21: An Exegesis by Michael Hardin." Lancaster: JDL, 2015.

———. "The Satan." *Preaching Peace* (May 2014). https://preachingpeace.org/the-satan/.

———. *What the Facebook? Posts from the Edge of Christendom*. Lancaster: JDL, 2014.

Harnack, Adolf von. *History of Dogma*. Translated by Neil Buchanan. Charleston: BiblioBazaar, 2007.

Hart, David Bentley. "God, Creation, and Evil: The Moral Meaning of creation ex nihilo." *Radical Orthodoxy: Theology, Philosophy, Politics*, Vol. 3, Number 1 (September 2015): 1–17.

Heim, Mark. *Saved from Sacrifice: A Theology of the Cross*. Grand Rapids: Eerdmans, 2006.

Hornblower, Simon and Spawforth, Antony, eds. *The Oxford Classical Dictionary: The Ultimate Reference Work on the Classical World*. 3rd Edition. Oxford: Oxford University Press, 1999.

Jersak, Brad. *A More Christlike God: A More Beautiful Gospel*. Pasadena: CWRpress, 2015.

———. "I Saw a Lamb: Interpreting 'Christ as the End' in the Apocalypse of John." In *The Jesus Driven Life: Reconnecting Humanity with Jesus*. 2nd Edition. Lancaster: JDL, 2013.

Jersak, Brad and Hardin, Michael, eds. *Stricken by God?: Nonviolent Identification and the Victory of Christ*. Grand Rapids: Eerdmans, 2007.

Jordan, Alexander M. "Universalism vs the Gospel." *Reforming Christianity* (October 2011). https://reformingchristianity.com/2011/10/08/universalism-vs-the-gospel/.

Julian of Norwich. *Revelations of Divine Love*. Mineola: Dover, 2006.

Kant, Immanuel. *Religion Within the Limits of Reason Alone*. Translated by Theodore M. Greene and Hoyt H. Hudson. New York: Harper & Row, 1960.

Lewis, C.S. *The Great Divorce*. St. Johns: Brawtley Press, 2014.

———. *The Problem of Pain*. Revised ed. Edition. San Francisco: HarperOne, 2015.

L'Engle, Madeleine. *A Stone for a Pillow*. Wheaton: Crosswicks, 1986.

Ludlow, Morwenna. "Universalism in the History of Christianity." In *Universal Salvation?: The Current Debate*. Edited by Robin Parry and Christopher Partridge. Grand Rapids: Eerdmans, 2003.

MacArthur, John. *The MacArthur New Testament Commentary: 1 Corinthians*. Chicago: Moody Press, 146.

MacDonald, George. "Justice." In *Unspoken Sermons*. http://georgemacdonald.info/justice.pdf.

Machuga, Ric. *Three Theological Mistakes: How to Correct Enlightenment Assumptions about God, Miracles, and Free Will*. Eugene: Cascade, 2015.

Mann, Jeffrey. "The Myth of a Non-Violent Jesus." *RealClear Religion* (April 2014). http://www.realclearreligion.org/articles/2014/04/30/the_myth_of_a_non-violent_jesus.html.

Marshall, Christopher D. *Beyond Retribution: A New Testament Vision for Justice, Crime, and Punishment*. Grand Rapids: Eerdmans, 2001.

Martyn, J. Louis. *Galatians: A New Translation with Introduction and Commentary*. New Haven: Yale University Press, 1997.

Miller, Caleb. *Saving God: Freeing Abba from the Captivity of Religion*. Fort Collins: Father's House, 2014.

Morrow, Carlotta. "Beware of Progressive Christianity: Jesus lovers are really Jesus haters." *Christocentric Press* (October 2011). http://christocentric.com/main/?p=3707.

Nelson, Caleb. "Marcion Lives! René Girard's Unoriginal Errors." *Juicy Ecumenism* (May 2013). https://juicyecumenism.com/2013/05/07/marcion-lives-rene-girards-unoriginal-errors/.

Olson, Roger. "How serious a heresy is universalism?" *Roger E. Olson* (July 2011). http://www.patheos.com/blogs/rogereolson/2011/07/how-serious-a-heresy-is-universalism/.

Patton, Michael. "Doubting Calvinist." *Credo House* (May 2013). http://credohouse.org/blog/doubting-calvinists.

Piper, John. "God's Wrath: 'Vengeance is Mine, I will Repay," Says the Lord. *Desiring God* (February 2005). http://www.desiringgod.org/messages/gods-wrath-vengeance-is-mine-i-will-repay-says-the-lord.

———. "Universalism and the Reality of Eternal Punishment: The Biblical Basis of the Doctrine of Eternal Punishment." *Desiring God* (January 1990). http://www.desiringgod.org/messages/universalism-and-the-reality-of-eternal-punishment-the-biblical-basis-of-the-doctrine-of-eternal-punishment.

Ramelli, Ilaria. *The Christian Doctrine of Apokatastasis: A Critical Assessment from the New Testament to Eriugena.* Leiden: Brill, 2013.

Reitan, Eric. "Human Freedom and the Impossibility of Eternal Damnation." In *Universal Salvation?: The Current Debate*, edited by Robin Parry and Christopher Partridge. Grand Rapids: Eerdmans, 2003.

Rohr, Richard. *Everything Belongs: The Gift of Contemplative Prayer.* New York: Crossroad, 2003.

Ross, Ashley. "Donald Trump Says He'd 'Take Out' Terrorists' Families." *Time* (December 2015). http://time.com/4132368/donald-trump-isis-bombing/.

Sanders, John. "A Freewill Theist's Response to Talbott's Universalism." In *Universal Salvation?: The Current Debate.* Edited by Robin Parry and Christopher Partridge. Grand Rapids: Eerdmans, 2003.

Shore, John. *Unfair: Christians and the LGBT Question.* John Shore, 2011.

Slick, Matt. "The Elements of Liberalism." *CARM.* https://carm.org/elements-liberalism

———. "What does the Bible say about homosexuality?" *CARM*. https://carm.org/bible-homosexuality.

———. "Substitutionary Atonement of Jesus Christ." *CARM* (December 2008). https://carm.org/substitutionary-atonement-jesus-christ.

Spira, Andreas and Klock, Christoph, eds. *Easter Sermons of Gregory of Nyssa: Translations and Commentary (Patristic Monography Series No. 9)*. Macon: Mercy University Press, 1981.

Talbott, Thomas. *The Inescapable Love of God*. 2nd Edition. Eugene: Cascade, 2014.

———. "Toward a Better Understanding of Universalism." In *Universal Salvation?: The Current Debate*, edited by Robin Parry and Christopher Partridge. Grand Rapids: Eerdmans, 2003.

Thomas, Geoff. "William Perkins on Assurance of Faith." *Banner of Truth* (December 2004). https://banneroftruth.org/us/resources/articles/2004/william-perkins-on-assurance-of-faith/.

Tolkien, J.R.R. *The Fellowship of the Ring*. New York: Ballantine, 1982.

Walls, Jerry. *Hell: The Logic of Damnation*. Notre Dame: University of Notre Dame Press, 1992.

Williams, Donald T. *Mere Humanity: G.K. Chesterton, C.S. Lewis, and J.R.R. Tolkien on the Human Condition*. Nashville: Broadman & Holman, 2006.

Williams, Rowan. *Being Christian: Baptism, Bible, Eucharist, Prayer*. Grand Rapids: Eerdmans, 2014.

Wright, N.T. *Surprised by Scripture: Engaging Contemporary Issues*. New York: HarperOne, 2014.

For more information about Matthew J. Distefano
or to contact him for speaking engagements,
please visit *www.allsetfree.com*

Many voices. One message.

Quoir is a boutique publishing company
with a single message: Christ is all.
Our books explore both His
cosmic nature and corporate expression.

For more information, please visit
www.quoir.com